Reflecting Easter

Living and Understanding the Resurrection

Stacy Voss

First Edition: March 2018.

ISBN: 1979551650

Cover design by tatlin.net.

DEDICATION

To Gabe and Micayla

Just like I can't comprehend the depths to which the Almighty loves me, my love for you runs deeper than you can imagine.

Shine, my little loves. Shine.

TABLE OF CONTENTS

ACKNOWLEDGMENTS

There are too many people who play such valuable roles in my life for me to name each and every one of you. You know who you are, my cheerleaders, my listeners, my hiking buddies and so much more. There are no words to describe how much I appreciate you.

Mom and Dad, you've spent more hours at my house than any of us care to calculate. You've torn down wallpaper, replaced floors (and pretty much everything else), jackhammered, textured and so much more. If it weren't for you, I'd still be covered in Kilz and wouldn't have had a chance to finish this book. You have taught me about unending love and transformation—and it has changed me in the process. Thank you!

Marsha, your keen eye caught more errors than I ever could have imagined. You promised you'd treat this project like it was your own and you fully delivered. Thank you for your encouragement, tenderness and tenacity.

I have no words to express my appreciation to my Launch Team. Judy Boyles, Christine Carter, Lynn Christensen, Lillian Friendt, Missy Goodenow, Linda Grand, Geri Harmony, Nancy Hollis, Robbie Iobst,

Suzanne Jewkes, Teresa Knapp, Kathy Merchant, Lenae Moore, Jessica Morley, Allie Slocum, Jan Sperry, AnneMarie Stone, Cara Venable and Kelly Winfrey, you all mean more to me than you'll ever know. Thank you!

PREFACE

Every year, I nearly miss it. I plan my little guy's birthday party, figure out what to do over spring break, maybe even cook up some corned beef for St. Patty's, but somehow, I almost forget Easter. It's not that I want to. After all, this is the defining moment of the Christian faith that sets our beliefs apart from all others. But maybe that's the unspoken problem: it's what sets us apart, and therefore the department stores don't start promoting it six months in advance like they do with Christmas.

But this isn't about blaming *them.* It's about *me*. There have been years I was more intentional in reflecting upon Easter and letting it's grandeur and sorrow penetrate deep. It did. Too much so, perhaps. The glory comes after a long string of pain, agony, wondering, desperation, abandonment and betrayal.

I experience those emotions much too frequently in this crazy and hard thing we call life. I dared not sign up to fully delve into them in order to truly reflect upon

Easter, so I let the days race by, living in the now of the birthday and spring break planning and only clicking the on button moments before we exuberantly cried out "He's alive!" Easter morning.

I thought I was protecting myself. At least that's what I attempted to convince that inner voice that beckoned me to lean in deeper to the angst of the season in order to better understand the full glory and hope it offers. Even as I write these words, I'm not sure I want to dive in that fully. The horror of the Easter story bring me to tears, but right as the floodgate is about to fully erupt, I pull back, switching channels as effortlessly as one surfing the TV.

Perhaps it is because I am coming out of a season of emotional and physical death of things held dear that I can more fully recognize that by embracing the wretchedness of certain aspects of life, I get to appreciate the grandeurs in ways I never could have imagined. Or maybe it's because I've walked through things unthinkable and, by God's limitless grace and the countless prayers of many cherished friends, I'm still alive and kicking.

The sorrow doesn't have to kill.

So, yes, we will dig into anguish. I won't promise this will be a light and fun journey, for how could one ever offer that when talking about the brutal killing of our Lord and Savior? But I can promise you this: by reflecting upon the agony and tackling the tough questions such as *why did Christ have to suffer?,* or perhaps the ones that ring truer, *why do we have to suffer?,* we will come to understand the greatest story ever lived.

But it won't end there. It's impossible to reflect *upon* Easter and all of its hardships without letting it reflect *in* and *through* us.

How to Use This Book

You'll notice that I didn't date each of the devotions. The reason is simple: Easter falls on a different date each year. Day 1 is designed to be started on Ash Wednesday so that Day 40 coincides with Easter. Days 41-50 give us a little extra time to process the resurrection and unpack how it applies to our daily lives.

SECTION I

UNDERSTANDING THE RESURRECTION

DAY 1. RACING PAST THE UNKNOWN

"How many more days?" I'd ask my co-worker, Stephanie, whenever she walked by my office. I didn't need to define the "until" part of the question because everyone knew what she was counting down to: the day she would be joined in matrimony with her beloved.

The months passed quickly (for us bystanders at least) and suddenly we were speaking about her wedding in the past tense.

"I can't believe how much everyone wants me to jump to the next thing," Stephanie told me a few months after her big day. "We just got married and people are already asking when we are going to start a family."

This isn't unique to my coworker. In fact, I'd guess that most of us have experienced it or have unintentionally done it to someone else.

"People start asking about what they consider to be the next big thing because they don't know enough about your character or the everyday goings-on of your life to have any other point of reference," I told her. "They don't know what else to say, so they skip ahead."

A few months after that conversation I found myself in a version of what Stephanie experienced. Oddly enough, the very words I said to her earlier resonated in a different context, challenging me in ways I could not have imagined.

The not knowing
Can make us skip ahead

I don't like hanging out with pain. Even though Christ died years ago, stopping to consider everything he went through on my behalf still is too painful for me to bear and instead I want to race past it. But just like skipping ahead to the next season in someone else's life can be the result of not knowing them, glossing over the events of Jesus' death and instead racing to the glorious event of his resurrection might actually *keep* me from knowing Christ more fully.

Forfeiting the time to sit in the agony of Christ's death robs me of the chance to more fully comprehend the extravagance of His love and mercy. If I only allow myself to feel a shallow "He suffered a lot" sentiment, then I garner little more than a "Jesus loves us" cliché that covers mankind. But if I stop pushing back the tears and instead let them drench my cheeks, the profound riches of something too incredible to comprehend begins to penetrate deeper.

The choice is ours alone: we can skim past the pain or let it be a tool to teach us about the depths of a love that is offered to each of us personally.

PAUSE AND REFLECT

1. When my Black Lab, Bella, was young, I didn't give it any thought when she came to lie on the floor beside my bed each night. Now that arthritis riddles her body, it takes her at least ten minutes to climb the stairs. She places her front paws on the steps and tries to pull up the rest of her aching body. It can take at least a half a dozen tries before she successfully makes it up a single stair. By the time she makes it to the top, she is exhausted, huffing louder than someone who just finished a marathon. Knowing she endures such pain just to be with me is an overwhelming thought . . .and she's just a dog!

How does the fact that Christ endured pain intentionally for us affect you?

2. Standing at the cross, Jesus's mother did not know what would happen just a few short days later. Neither did the disciple John. When we are given a diagnosis that could prove fatal or are betrayed by a loved one, we only see today and cannot predict the events of tomorrow. As we embrace the "in-process-ness" of the

cross, our unknowns somehow make a little more sense. How might sitting in the pain of Good Friday bring you a clearer perspective about the things that are going on in your life today?

3. I have tutored numerous students throughout the years. There is a huge difference between kids who think they don't need help but simply tolerate my presence because their parents said they needed to be tutored and those who genuinely want to understand the subject but are struggling to learn. Give me a kid who will admit they don't understand the topic any day! If I feel that way about a person I am being paid to teach, think about how God must feel when we are totally honest and admit there is still so much more about Jesus that we don't understand, especially concerning the ways in which He loves us. Let me encourage you to take a few minutes (or the rest of your life) to ask Him to help you better understand Him and for God to reveal more of His love and character to you.

DAY 2. THE SEAT OF HUMILITY

On a beautiful spring day, my chemistry class went to our teacher's house to prepare for the upcoming advanced placement exam. We set up camp in her backyard, armed with blankets, textbooks, paper, pencil, and a fervor to do well enough on the test to get college credit.

We took a lunch break when the pizza we ordered arrived. Standing up for the first time all morning, we were shocked to discover there was something in the grass that stuck to our feet. We rinsed them with water from the hose, but the sap-like substance refused to come off.

When Mrs. Andrew saw that half of her backyard clung to our feet, she brought out buckets of warm water, soap, and washcloths. We scrubbed as hard as we could, but to no avail. We realized that the only way to get our feet clean was to sit in a lawn chair, prop one leg on someone else, and let them scrub with all their might. In a desperate attempt to get the goop off our feet, our A.P. cram-fest soon turned into a time of foot washing.

Others talked about how challenging it was to sit there and let others serve them. It wasn't until it was my turn that I could fully appreciate just how hard it really was. As one of the last to have my feet washed, I sat there and watched people (yes, plural) working with all of their might for my benefit while I tried not to squirm since I'm much too ticklish.

I appreciated their help, but I also felt defeated. After all, they could do something that I hadn't been able to accomplish on my own despite my greatest efforts.

We were supposed to learn chemistry that day, but the real lesson was about humility. I used to think the real humility came from Jesus' lack of pride, lowering himself to take on the position that was reserved for the lowest of the servants: the role of cleaning other people's feet. While this act indeed depicts Jesus' humility, it compels me for yet another reason: it reminds me that in order to fully receive His sacred act of selflessly paying the ultimate price for me, I must first recognize how little I can do on my own and humbly accept His gift while realizing I would never obtain its benefits on my own.

Maybe the challenge of allowing someone to give me what I'm unable to get for myself is why I prefer to let Easter be just a story, a far-off intellectual thing rather than something my heart wrestles through. The emotions, the agony, the angst of what He did for me put me back in that chair, sitting there helplessly while someone empties themself on my behalf. Just like that sap, I have something on me I can't get rid of without the help of another, so I sit in the seat of humility and thank Jesus for His gift. I hope you'll join me.

PAUSE AND REFLECT

1. Have you ever been in a situation where you tried doing something on your own but failed miserably? Did you have a better outcome once you let someone help you?

2. Do you have a hard time believing that the gift of Easter—the cleansing of your sins through the blood of Jesus—could only be accomplished through something that you have no ability to impact?

3. Serving another in a humble fashion forms a powerful bond. In fact, when I bumped into a former classmate eighteen years later, we still talked about our unplanned foot washing ceremony. Have you allowed the humility of Jesus serving you draw you closer to Him? Have you been able to humble yourself to allow

Him to see who you truly are, messes and all (between you and me, I have a feeling He's pretty familiar with them already!)?

DAY 3. THE LAST LECTURE

"Mr. Hollis, this is Sally from St. Joseph's Hospital. Your mom took a turn for the worse and we think you should get here as quickly as you can."

It was December 24th. My parents and I packed our bags and headed to the airport. We waited in line with Christmas travelers eager to see loved ones. Ours was not one of long-awaited anticipation. We just hoped we'd make it there in time.

We did.

Gratefully.

We leaned in close, ready to listen. Grandma said something to my mom and dad, at least I imagine she did. I really don't remember. All I can recall are the words she spoke to me, an encouragement that was well-meaning but misplaced. Because of her failing health, my parents and I decided not to tell her about the life events I was experiencing. Without that information, she encouraged me to make a decision that could potentially be extremely damaging for me.

Later that night my dad quietly said to me "Stacy, you can't bind yourself to what she asked of you. She never would have said it had she realized what was going on." They were words of wisdom coming from someone who was looking out for me. Dad knew the need to override Grandma's words because he has been on this earth long enough to know that when someone utters their last words, we listen intently and then take action. Some of us will even let those words define the rest of our days, our living determined by the non-living.

> Some of us let someone's final words define the rest of our days, our living determined by the non-living.

There is a special reverence given to final words, those last utterances a loved one feels compelled to say to us while they still can. We watched it with Randy Pausch, the professor from Carnegie Mellon University who knew he was dying of cancer. While appearing healthy but fully aware of his impending mortality, he shared his *Last Lecture* with students and faculty. We, too, listened in as a country, placing his book on the New York Times Bestseller list and watching him on various television shows.

Why?

Because final words matter greatly, ones that look back to set things straight and those reaching forward hoping to point and direct.

Friend, it's time for us to lean in even closer and listen. I'm not about to undermine any of the words Jesus said at any point in his lifetime, but I can't help but believe that the things he said during his last week of life reflect many of the issues he most wanted us to grasp.

During Holy Week, Jesus spoke of forgiveness and his authority. He broke bread in a much gentler manner than the ways in which his body would be broken. He walked directly and intentionally to the place he knew he'd be arrested. He warned us to "be careful, or your hearts will be weighed down with dissipation, drunkenness, and the anxieties of life" (Luke 21:34a).

The words Jesus spoke during his final week have tremendous, life-altering implications if we allow them to penetrate our hearts. Let's lean in and listen.

PAUSE AND REFLECT

1. Has anyone encouraged or challenged you from their deathbed? If so, how did their words impact you?

2. Have you ever let the non-living affect your living? What happened?

3. There is no way we'll be able to explore everything Jesus said and did during his "Last Lecture." However, if you are familiar with some of the things he said or did during that period, which holds the most meaning for you? Why?

DAY 4. THE NECESSITY OF SUFFERING

"Gabe and Micayla, I want you guys to clean your room while I run to the store, okay?"

"Sure, Mom," they chime in that sing-song way that causes me to question if their room will look any better once I lug in groceries.

Now compare that request to the times when I'm tired of tripping over things and their mess is more than I can stand.

"Listen up. You must clean your room while I'm gone, or else you'll lose your electronics for a week."

This time I leave knowing their room will be as close to spotless as possible. Why? Because I said they must do it and give an enforceable consequence if they opt for anything other than compliance.

Easter follows the second option. It was the real-life version of "You must do this or else." But there is one significant difference: the One who issued the ultimatum said *he* had to do something or *others* would pay the consequences.

> "For the Son of Man in his day will be like the lightning, which flashes and lights up the sky from one end to the other. But first he must suffer many things and be rejected by this generation." Luke 17:24-25

You'll find this text in red letters in the Bible because this is Jesus talking. Soak that in for a minute, Jesus saying, "The Son of Man **must** suffer many things and be rejected." The original Greek text used the word "*dei*" meaning "must" (not to be confused with *imago dei,* the Latin phrase meaning the "image of God"). *Dei* is a strong word meaning "of divine importance, of great necessity."

Translation: it was divinely important and necessary for Jesus to suffer.

> Jesus said it was divinely important for Him to suffer.

Looking through a human lens, that's nonsensical and counter-intuitive. We wouldn't willingly sign up for a round of suffering, let alone decree that it was of great importance. My human mind can't comprehend it because it is just that: human. But Jesus, in his humanity *and* diety, willingly chose to subject himself to the most intense form of suffering.

It leaves me scratching my head, perplexed beyond words. I want to ask why, but honestly I'm scared to ask because the answer cuts to the quick.

"You want to know why, Stacy," He whispers gently. "*Because you were the consequence. You could never join me in heaven if I hadn't suffered."*

Oh, mercy! My heart tries to brush it off and skip over this radical reality. Jesus suffered, for me. For you. Not the kind of suffering that comes as a result of someone else's actions, but the kind that is even more unthinkable: the intentional, purposeful suffering that is experienced for the benefit of another.

Throughout the gospels we hear the screams of anguish and cringe at the thought of flesh being ripped and torn. Listen in even closer and you'll also hear another sound: the answer to the call of the necessity of suffering.

PAUSE AND REFLECT

1. Do you agree that Jesus had to suffer? Can you think of an alternative, if any, where Jesus could have achieved the same goal of our salvation without enduring the cross?

2. What impact does *dei* have on you as you recognize that Jesus said it was divinely important for him to suffer?

3. How does the divine importance of Jesus' suffering make you feel about the trials you may have faced in your life?

DAY 5. IMPROMPTU EUPHORIA

There are two things I haven't outgrown from my younger days: my prom dress and Palm Sunday. It's dumb luck that the dress still fits, but I'm grateful to still view Palm Sunday with the same childlike awe I did so many years ago.

Mrs. Mannis, my Sunday-school teacher, handed me and every kid at our church a palm branch. I traipsed into church, many times in my boots on snowy Palm Sundays, always amazed to be holding a branch that came from somewhere warm and tropical. Holding that branch, my heart started filling with a sense of awe and great anticipation.

"Okay, kids, come up to the stage," Mrs. Mannis would say.

We'd rush on up, for there was no time to waste. We knew what was coming.

Not what. *Who.*

There, in the front of my church, "Jesus" passed by. I can't remember if someone donned a costume from the Christmas pageant wardrobe or if a person in street clothes walked past us. All I remember is waving my palm branch while shouting, "Hosanna! Hosanna! Save us, Jesus, save. Hosanna." Tears would well in my eyes, brimming with the immense pride that I somehow got to play a part in honoring the Most High. Oh yes, Hosanna. Save me, my Lord. From you comes salvation.

Palm Sunday looked a bit goofy, people grabbing at the closest thing possible to turn the common into a thing of worship.

Decades later, the euphoria of Palm Sunday still brings me great joy mixed with bittersweet tears. The day catches me off guard. *Can it really be Palm Sunday already?* I wonder as I finish getting kids and myself ready and rush out the door to worship. Ours is an impromptu celebration, offering mere breaths of gratitude compared to what should have been given.

Perhaps that's what Palm Sunday really was—and is—an unplanned time to stop and say thanks. No one expected to grab whatever was closest to them and turn it into a way to praise another. There are multiple theories about the reasons behind Palm Sunday. Some say it stemmed from an ancient practice of welcoming a hero or king by laying branches for them to ride on. Others attribute it to the Romans who honored champions of athletic games with palm branches. And then there's the interpretation I heard most recently that stirred something deep: it was a sudden reaction to the euphoria of being in the presence of the Most High. Bystanders didn't have time to run home to gather their best party things or to spread fliers letting others know about a set time of celebration. Nope. It was an instantaneous overflowing of joy as people grabbed whatever was closest to them and turned it into a thing of worship.

Just like the original Palm Sunday was unscripted, it can remain so today. Grab the branch right now. Don't put a time of worship and celebration on the calendar, adding another to-do item to the list. Stop. Right now. Even if it feels as foreign as a palm branch in Colorado, grab it and send shouts of praise and adoration to Him who sits on the throne.

PAUSE AND REFLECT

1. Do you have any Palm Sunday memories? If so, what are they?

2. Have you ever seen others erupt into sudden, euphoric praise? Perhaps it was a standing ovation after a concert or parents cheering as their daughter took her first steps. How did it affect you? What impact did it have on the recipient?

3. Palm Sunday looked a bit goofy, people grabbing at the closest item possible to turn the common into a thing of worship. We tend to sterilize our worship, tuning it down so it looks appropriate, or dodging some of the hardest truths of the Bible for fear of the deep-reaching impacts it might have. Leave "appropriate" behind and in it's place offer impromptu praise.

DAY 6. LEARNING TO TRUST

My Girlie asked me to help her get ready for her Spanish quiz.

"Okay. *Como te llamas*?" I asked with a slow drawl so she could understand my words.

"No, Mom! I'm not supposed to be able to speak it. I have to learn to write the words and spell them properly."

"If you can first pronounce the words, it'll make it easier to spell them."

"But you're doing it wrong," she protested. I chose to dismiss the irony that she complained about not being able to learn based on the way her teacher taught it but then got upset that I wasn't teaching it the same way.

"I need you to trust me, okay?"

"Yes, but you don't understand . . ."

"I'm asking you to trust me," I repeated with enough gusto that she knew to stop and hear me out. "I need you to believe that I know you well enough to understand how you learn. I also want you to remember that I'm bilingual and that I tutor other kids, including in Spanish. This might not feel like you're learning what you need to at first, but will you trust me to teach you?"

"Okay," she quietly responded.

For thirty minutes, I asked her questions in Spanish as I pulled weeds.

Will you let me teach you in the way that I know is best for you?

"*¿Tienes un hermano?* (Do you have a brother?)

"*Si, tengo un hermano.*"

Most of the time she obliged me with an answer, although a few times she stopped to remind me that she needed to memorize the sentences describing herself and her family and know how to spell everything. Regardless of her comments, we kept trekking along.

Until.

"Mom, can you just quiz me and see how much of this I memorized?" she asked.

"Okay. How about you go inside and write it out."

A few minutes later, she handed me the paragraph. In Spanish. With 1 letter off on a word and another missing an accent. Coming from the girl who constantly makes spelling mistakes in English.

I wanted to say, "See. I told you so," but before it escaped my mouth, a question penetrated to the marrow.

"Will you trust me?"

Huh?

"Stacy, do you believe I know you well enough to understand how you learn? Will you let me teach you in the way I know is best for you?"

Egads! The rare and quiet voice of God, prodding deep, laid to rest many of my questions about why I had to endure the trials I had recently gone through.

As I recounted this story to a friend, I cried out, "and here I was thinking we were just learning about verbs."

"You were," she replied. "The verb is trust."

Listen in, for that same verb rings out throughout the Easter story. It's about the trust of a son to take his father at his word and believe he would bring him back to life. Jesus believed that despite the curse of the cross, His Father, God Almighty, would once again lavish His love upon Him. It's about the trust that His ultimate sacrifice would compel us to do just that: trust.

PAUSE AND REFLECT

1. What is your learning style? Do you do best when you see something, experiment with it hands-on, write it out, etc.?

2. A ruler addressed Jesus as the good teacher (Luke 18:18). Do you believe He is a good teacher? Why or

why not? If you believe He is a good teacher, do you believe He knows you well enough to teach you in the best possible way?

3. What are some of the ways that you see the verb of trust written into the Easter story, perhaps in the narrative of Jesus' life and death, or maybe also in the story of how you reflect Easter in your thoughts and beliefs?

DAY 7. SPRING CLEANING

It's the time of year most of us look forward to. The snow melts, the grass greens, and nature awakens. But with it comes that dreaded thing that looms large: Spring Cleaning!

You know the drill. Windows are popped out of their sills to get them more pristine than the day they were installed. Toys are donated. Clothes are tried on to determine if they still fit and if they are worth keeping. Cobwebs are swept away and closets are reorganized.

It is a time to purge, get rid of the clutter, and remove the things that hinder the way for the new life that's about to spring forth. It's a routine that dates back to Jesus' day. In fact, the second recorded spring cleaning happened the day after Jesus triumphantly entered the City of Jerusalem (the Triumphal Entry).

Jesus walked into the temple in Jerusalem, the sacred place built to honor his Father. Instead of finding glimpses of reverence, he found animal droppings. Vendors sold birds and lambs for others to sacrifice and money changers lined the hallways. It was turned into a commercial environment instead of one consisting of worship and prayer.

When I read this I picture the busy Mexican markets I've grown to love.

"Get your doves here," one man calls out.

"I have the best lambs in town. Guaranteed to bring pardon for your sins," another one cries over the throng.

The sacred was a supermarket.

Until spring cleaning, that is. Yes, the animal droppings needed to go, but so did those who were profiting off the people who wanted to serve and worship God. And go, they did. In a magnificent moment of righteous anger, Jesus overturned the merchants' tables and scattered the money changers' coins.

> "On reaching Jerusalem, Jesus entered the temple courts and began driving out those who were buying and selling there. He overturned the tables of the money changers and the benches of those selling doves, and would not allow anyone to carry merchandise through the temple courts. And as he taught them, he said, "Is it not written: 'My house will be called a house of prayer for all nations'? But you have made it 'a den of robbers.'"
> Mark 11:15-17

Jesus didn't just clean out the temple that day. He also cleansed my perception of Him. It's safer to view

Him being like a koala bear who has been munching on so much eucalyptus that he's sweet, gentle, and extremely passive. But these verses won't let me hold on to this myth. Instead I see images of a powerful, commanding Jesus, the One I love, forcibly removing and cleaning what is unholy from His Father's house.

"Get out of here!"

"How dare you!"

Can't you see mothers drawing their children close, money changers trying to grab their coins before Jesus pushes over their tables scattering all their profits? Do you hear the animals blaahing and bleeting as merchants frantically try to corral them?

No fog-inducing eucalyptus leaves here. Instead we see a zeal, a passion, a purpose, and a drive to do what needed to be done. It wasn't the only time Jesus cleaned out the temple. We find the first encounter in John 2:14-15:

> "In the temple courts he found people selling cattle, sheep and doves, and others sitting at tables exchanging money. *So he made a whip out of cords,* and drove all from the temple courts, both sheep and cattle; he scattered the coins of the money changers and overturned their tables" (emphasis mine).

Just like spring cleaning is an annual event, there might be thought patterns we've worked to purge from our lives, only to discover they're back in force. Perhaps it's the way we view others. Maybe it's the negative words we say about ourselves, or possibly our perception of Christ is distorted. Whatever the case, let's commit to doing some spring cleaning today by praying that God remove anything in our thoughts or lives that keeps us from fully serving Him.

PAUSE AND REFLECT

1. Do you have a spring cleaning regimen? If so, what are some of the things you do?

2. Do you typically view Jesus more as the gentle koala, the whip-cracking spring cleaner, or something else? What do you think causes that perception of Him?

3. How does knowing that Jesus responded in ways that may seem un-Christ-like affect you? Does it make you want to do some spring cleaning of your own as you toss out faulty perceptions you have of Christ and make room for the truth about our living God?

DAY 8. GOD AND CAESAR

I have to give my ex-husband a copy of my financial statements by May 1st. A few days beforehand, I started making copies of bank statements and tax returns, checking each item off the list until only one thing remained: a state tax return.

You would think it would be easy to find just a few weeks after it was due, but I could not lay my hands on it. I scanned files on my computer and rummaged through every folder in my filing cabinet. I found receipts from years ago and dust bunnies in places I'd rather not mention, but that tax return was nowhere to be found.

You know why?

Because I completely spaced doing it.

My oversight embarrasses me to no end. After all, who *doesn't* file their tax returns, or at least request an extension?

It's unthinkable to me to not report my earnings. I'm not about to mess with the IRS.

In Jesus' final week before the crucifixion, some men tried to trap Jesus by using His own words against

Him (although I would think the wisest of men would try to avoid this at all costs).

> "Teacher, we know that you speak and teach what is right, and that you do not show partiality but teach the way of God in accordance with the truth. Is it right for us to pay taxes to Caesar or not?" Luke 20:21-22

Jesus, of course, saw beyond their question knowing what they were trying to do. Instead of saying He was for or against Caesar, He responded with the following words many of us have heard before:

> "Show me a denarius. Whose image and inscription are on it?
>
> "Caesar's, they replied.
>
> "He said to them, "Then give to Caesar what is Caesar's, and to God what is God's." Luke 20:24-25

And so I give to the government what belongs to the government. At least I usually do, not counting the year I forgot (which I immediately corrected, by the way). Yet even though all my taxes are now current, I'm still accountable for only partially obeying this command.

You see, I give Uncle Sam his share. The horror stories my friends have shared after being audited is enough to make sure I keep giving "Caesar" what I am required to give. Yet I still complete only a portion of this two-sided-equation, Too often I forget the most important part, to give to God what is due Him. Sure, I praise Him, especially on the good days when things are going well, but do I really give God what is His?

To answer that, I need to define what is God's. The first thing that comes to mind is me. Here's the spoiler alert: Jesus died on the cross. We are intimately familiar with that truth, yet its reality should impact our everyday living. If God gave His own son to die for me then is it too much to ask for my whole being in return?

Absolutely not.

Even if I surrender all that I am for all time, it still falls short when compared to the cost of the gift given for me. Despite my awareness of this truth, I shortchange Him when I get so caught up in the things happening around me that I lose my focus and stop giving Him me.

I want to come to a place where such a mindset is even more unthinkable than calling the government taxing authorities to verify receipt of my tax return (and trust me, I'll do whatever I can to keep from repeating that experience).

So why is it that I so easily forget what Jesus said about giving to God what is God's, much more easily than I did my tax return that year?

All honor and glory is due Him. Overdue, in fact.

PAUSE AND REFLECT

1. Would you ever consider not filing a tax return if you knew you were supposed to? Why or why not?

2. How would you rate yourself at giving God what is due Him? This isn't meant to criticize or condemn, but simply to serve as a challenge for us to dig deeper, pause a little longer, and give more praise to "Him who is able to do immeasurably more than all we can ask, think or imagine" (Ephesians 3:20).

3. Think about three things God has done for you lately. Stop right now and give God the glory due Him by thanking Him for those things.

DAY 9. CORRECTING THE ERROR

As is our custom, I asked my little guy, “How was school today?”

“Well,” he paused thoughtfully, a telling sign since my Bubba is known to spout off every detail of recess and who he played with. “Ms. Smith had me go up to the board and share my answer from a math problem,” he said, his voice dropping lower in sadness.

“And you didn’t know how to solve it?” I asked.

“No, Mom. I knew the answer, but I couldn’t explain how I got it. It was so embarrassing.”

I reassured him that since he knew the answer, he probably understood how to solve it.

“It was just so embarrassing standing there and not knowing how to do it,” he said again.

There’s no arguing that. Who wants to make it known that they don’t fully understand something, especially when others are watching?

I sure don’t, even though I frequently find myself in that position. I have a feeling I’m not alone. Even some of the religious leaders in Jesus' day were sheep-faced after being told of their error in front of others.

Two days after Jesus' Triumphal Entry, some Sadducees asked Jesus who a certain woman would be married to in heaven.

> "Jesus replied, 'You are in error because you do not know the Scriptures or the power of God. At the resurrection people will neither marry nor be given in marriage; they will be like the angels in heaven" Matthew 22:29-30

My brain can comprehend His answer, that there will be no marriage in heaven (this divorcee is quite glad for that!), but the first half of His response stops me in my tracks: "You are in error because you do not know the Scriptures or the power of God."

The next morning I drilled my little guy on math facts as we drove to school. Thinking he was catching me and without having done anything wrong, he said, "Mom, you can ground me for as many days as eight times eight."

"You want me to ground you for sixty-four days? That's more than two months!"

"Huh?" he questioned. "Oh, wait! I meant eight *divided* by eight!"

"That's one. Do you want me to ground you for a day?"

"No! I meant eight divided by *zero!"*

Being in error can be costly, especially when our error is failing to grasp the power of the Scriptures.

PAUSE AND REFLECT

1. Have you ever been called on but didn't know the answer? If so, how did it make you feel?

2. How would you feel if you believed something with everything in you, only to discover that you barely knew it at all or were completely off in your perception?

3. Imagine believing in Jesus and following Him every day for the rest of your life. How would you feel if, when you meet Him face to face, He said you were in error for not believing the power of God?

4. Do you think it likely that Jesus would tell you that you are in error when it comes to your understanding of the power of God? If so, what can you do to help change that? I'll get you started with my suggestion:

Oh, God, so often I think I understand, but you and I both know how clueless I really am about how great and powerful you are. Please remind me yet again of the truth about your love and power, and help me embrace it, believe it, and live with the knowledge that there is nothing too hard for you.
Amen.

DAY 10. THE TIMELINE OF TRUST

"When will your next book come out?" the radio broadcaster asked.

I hadn't expected the question. Then again, I had come to realize that nothing was predictable with that particular radio show.

"A few months before next Easter," I responded, referring to the book you are holding in your hands.

That was two years ago. I fully meant it when I said it would be available by then, especially since I was seventy percent done with the first draft. Little did I know that life would take a few more unexpected turns and margins would get squeezed out. I had to choose between my already inadequate amounts of sleep or finishing this project.

Okay, let's be real. For me it wasn't a choice. I love sleep even more than chocolate! So the well-intentioned words I said that day on the radio—and which were broadcast around the area and online—ended up being false and untrue.

Gulp. I seriously hate breaking my promises and despise sharing a timeframe that ends up being off by a factor of years. Talk about major embarrassment!

Perhaps that is why the following verses baffle me in a way I can't fully articulate. Jesus said to His disciples, "As you know, the Passover is two days away—and the Son of Man will be handed over to be crucified" (Matthew 26:2).

T minus two and counting. Ready for the astounding part?

> "Then the chief priests and the elders of the people assembled in the palace of the high priest, whose name was Caiaphas, and they plotted to arrest Jesus in some sly way and kill him." Matthew 26:3-4

Are you tracking with this timeline? Jesus said He would be crucified in two days *and then* people began plotting how to kill Him. Judas hadn't made arrangements to betray Jesus with the chief priests, nor had talks begun about arresting Him.

I have no experience with plotting to kill someone, but I would assume it typically takes weeks or even months. In fact, the trial process alone in that region should have been prolonged to take days or weeks. It simply wasn't heard of for someone to be arrested and executed in a matter of hours.

My first thought is that perhaps Jesus could have avoided being crucified if He hadn't said anything. Of course, I have to eliminate that notion since He was aware that the cross—and our eternal lives!—were the very reasons He came to earth.

My second thought, the one that sticks around longer as it settles in deep, begins with the scene my mind conjures up if I had been in Jesus' sandals:

"God, I know I'm supposed to be crucified, but these people haven't even started talking about how they're going to arrest me. Do I really want to give people a specific day as to when it will happen? What if I just say I will be crucified, but don't put it on the calendar to give people time to start planning?"

That right there is reason 1,000,094 why I'm me and not Jesus. You see, I'm a planner, which is my excuse for saying that for me to believe something *will* happen, I first need the evidence that it is *already* starting.

But not Jesus. I'm not saying He didn't plan, for He wouldn't have walked this earth if the plan for His death hadn't already been made. My point is simply this: Jesus could put a definitive timeline on things that no one else had even pondered because He fully trusted His Father.

It's like when a client asked my employee and I if we could produce something a week earlier than promised. My employee, who I entrusted this project to, said she could do it. I wouldn't have hired her if I didn't know without a doubt that if she said we would be able to deliver, she would deliver. Why? Because my employee is trustworthy.

But we aren't talking simply about a timeline here that could potentially dampen Jesus' testimony if it didn't come true. It was literally a matter of life and death. Even so—*especially* so!—it could still be entrusted to God.

I don't know about you, but that sure rattles and strengthens my timeline of trust.

PAUSE AND REFLECT

1. Have you ever promised something based on a certain timeline and not been able to deliver? How did that make you feel? How does the possibility of not completing something on time affect the way you set deadlines?

2. What does Jesus' announcement about His death being two days away teach you about His trust in God?

3. What is one small thing you can do today to move towards having more faith, even in (or especially so) the things that seemingly don't have any precursors in

place? Perhaps it is simply praying, “I do believe; help me overcome my unbelief!" (Mark 9:24)

DAY 11. THE BEAUTY OF THE UNTHINKABLE

You most likely know about Mary from the Mary and Martha story in the Bible (Luke 10:38-42). She was the sitter, the one who chose to be present with Jesus and savor the moment, while her sister, Martha, was preoccupied with the many tasks at hand.

In this story we see the busy be (as in 'be' in the presence of the Almighty) and the busy bee.

One day Jesus ate in the home of Simon the Leper (or as I would name him, Simon the once-leper since Jesus cured him completely of that highly contagious disease).

> "While Jesus was in Bethany in the home of Simon the Leper, a woman came to him with an alabaster jar of very expensive perfume, which she poured on his head as he was reclining at the table.
>
> When the disciples saw this, they were indignant. 'Why this waste?' they asked. 'This perfume could

> have been sold at a high price and the money given to the poor.'" Matthew 26:6-9

John 12:3 names the woman, our main character, in his telling of this story:

> "Here a dinner was given in Jesus' honor. Martha served, while Lazarus was among those reclining at the table with him. Then Mary took about a pint of pure nard, an expensive perfume; she poured it on Jesus' feet and wiped his feet with her hair. And the house was filled with the fragrance of the perfume." John 12:2-3

Can you picture the scene? Jesus is eating at the house of Simon the (once) Leper, with Lazarus (the man who was once dead until Jesus called him back to life) when Mary pours an expensive perfume on Jesus' feet. I imagine several people in the room were confused and bewildered by what was going on, but in my mind's eye, I picture Simon and Lazarus on the brink of getting up to join Mary at His feet as a result of their gratitude and affection when Judas interjects,

> First someone condemned Mary for *not* doing something. Later, she was questioned because she *was* doing something.

> "Why wasn't this perfume sold and the money given to the poor? It was worth a year's wages." John 12:5

Oh, poor Mary. Here we go again. First, someone condemned her for *not* doing something. Later, another questioned her because she *was* doing something. In neither case did Mary need to respond or justify her actions, especially since Jesus spoke truth into each of these situations. When Martha tattled to Jesus about her do-nothing sister, Jesus replied, "Mary has chosen what is better, and it will not be taken away from her" Luke 10:42. In the instance with the oil, Jesus answered,

> "The poor you will always have with you, and you can help them whenever you want. But you will not always have Me. She has done what she could to anoint My body in advance of My burial. And truly I tell you, wherever the gospel is preached in all the world, what she has done will also be told in memory of her." Mark 14:7-9

Martha was well-meaning and wanted what was best for Jesus. The same could be said about the disciples (minus Judas). In both of these events, Mary was in good company, surrounded by people who loved and adored the same Savior as she. And yet both times words of criticism arose as a direct result of what she did or did not do. Despite the rebukes (or perhaps because of them), Jesus affirms Mary's actions by acknowledging and praising the beauty of what others considered to be the unthinkable. Oh, that today and forevermore we can do what others think is irresponsible if it means doling out gratitude and adoration to the One most deserving of it.

PAUSE AND REFLECT

1. Does it seem necessary for someone to pour a perfume so expensive that it cost a year's worth of wages onto Jesus' feet? Why or why not?

2. There are countless times when a Christ-follower sets out to do something, only to have other believers make fun of them or find reasons to talk them out of it. If you have been on either side of that equation, how do Jesus' responses about Mary challenge you?

3. While others criticized Mary, part of Jesus' response was, "she did what she could." You and I can't pour perfume on Jesus' feet and we might not be able to buy something costing our annual salary, but there is still something we can do to give praise to Jesus. What can you do?

If you haven't done it yet, when will you? If you're anything like me, you'll need to be specific as to the who, what, when and where if you want to follow through on doing what you can.

DAY 12. THE CERTAINTY OF THE UNCERTAIN

"Do you think we should actually go through with this?"

"I don't know. It sounds a little nuts if you ask me."

"Not just a little," the first man replies with a chuckle. "Oh, well. Let's give it a shot."

You won't find this little interchange in the Bible, yet I wouldn't be surprised if some variation of it occurred between the words that were penned in Luke 22:7-12:

> “Then came the day of Unleavened Bread on which the Passover lamb had to be sacrificed. Jesus sent Peter and John, saying, 'Go and make preparations for us to eat the Passover.'
>
> 'Where do you want us to prepare for it?’ they asked.

> He replied, 'As you enter the city, a man carrying a jar of water will meet you. Follow him to the house that he enters, and say to the owner of the house, 'The Teacher asks: Where is the guest room, where I may eat the Passover with my disciples?' He will show you a large room upstairs, all furnished. Make preparations there.'" Luke 22:7-12

Whoa! Say what? Go look for a *man* carrying a jar of water? Women were in charge of that task. The footnote in my NIV Bible says it'd be extraordinary to find a man carrying water.

Translation: "Peter and John, go find something that never happens. Follow the person doing the unheard of act and ask for something even more rare: for use of a guest room that is set for you. He'll show it to you, all ready to go."

I wonder if those fishermen thought something was fishy, or if their years with Jesus allowed them to walk with certainty towards something that most would consider preposterous.

I can't begin to say since the Bible doesn't share any of that, but this I know:

> "They left and found things just as Jesus had told them." Luke 22:13

It bears repeating: just as He told them.

This somewhat insignificant scene usually falls to the background in my mind as I attempt to grapple with all of the events leading up to Easter. This uncertainty is but a blip in the drama.

Or is it?

I've wrestled with more unknowns this past year than I ever have previously. How will I make ends meet? How can I work, be available for my kids, and still have margins to write and speak? On and on the questions loomed, the answers far-off and unknown.

As I read Luke 22 this morning, the waves of uncertainty still infiltrating my thoughts, "just as He told him" took on greater relevance than ever before. The thing that perhaps seemed preposterous to Peter and John simply *was* to Jesus. *Was* as in, was fact, was do-able, and was already in the works before He even gave voice to it.

My Girlie was crying yesterday because some rumors were being spread about her. "Your friends won't believe any of what's being said if it's contrary to your character," I assured her. That's what the time-tested version of trust does for a relationship.

It's the very same thing with Jesus.

If He could promise there'd be a man carrying water, then guess what? There was a man!

If He could promise said man would show them to the place where they'd prepare the Passover, then there'd be a place.

And if He promised He'd never leave us nor forsake us (Hebrews 13:5), well, you know the answer, right? Or perhaps you're more like me, with our heads knowing what our hearts fear to embrace.

I don't know if Peter and John walked into town with certainty, confusion or fear. In fact, we probably don't know because it isn't important. The fact is, they embraced the certainty of the uncertain and had their faith boosted along the way.

Oh, that we may follow their footsteps.

PAUSE AND REFLECT

1. Is it hard to believe something that seems preposterous, especially in uncertain times? How have you learned to walk in faith when things are unknown and foreign?

2. Indulge me for a minute and jot down the number for the month you were born (i.e. 1 for January, 5 for May, etc.). Next to it write the number of kids you have or would like to have. Now write the year you were born, followed by your street number. You should have enough numbers to represent a phone number (and if not, feel free to add some of your choosing).

Would you believe me if I said to dial that number right now, ask for $1,000, and the person on the other end would automatically give it to you? (if by some chance this happens to work, feel free to share your winnings with me!).

3. Is there something you feel like God is prompting you to do, perhaps even something that seems ridiculous or impossible to most? If so, what is keeping you from it?

.

DAY 13. A GIFT TO THE UNDESERVING

"It doesn't matter what I get them, they're still going to complain," my daughter said of some people in her life. Their affluence made it possible for them to buy anything they desired and their bitterness made it hard for them to appreciate the things she gave them—items she spent days preparing since she would make presents in order to stretch her limited resources.

"I just don't want to give them anything this year," she said quietly. "It just hurts too much."

As a mom, perhaps I should have condoned her attitude, but I couldn't since I could relate. It's hard to give a gift when you know beyond a doubt that it won't be received in the vein it is given.

I think we could end this book right here, for that sentiment fully encapsulates Easter and the gospel message. But let's break it down some more to glean more of its richness.

Take, for example, the Last Supper. Some have called it ordinary while others deem it extraordinary. I happen to think it has elements of both, beginning with the extraordinary parts we looked at yesterday when Peter and John went out in search of the upper room and found it—*just as He had said!* There was the extraordinary of Jesus washing the disciples' feet, an act that was reserved for the lowest of slaves to perform.

We see some of the ordinary, too, as these men shared yet another meal together. This wasn't a stuffy dinner on fancy china with everyone sitting in a tense, rigid position. No, sir. Luke 22:14 paints the picture of Jesus and His disciples reclining at the table. And then, an unthinkable gift given to all, including the undeserving:

> "When the hour came, Jesus and his apostles reclined at the table. And he said to them, 'I have eagerly desired to eat this Passover with you before I suffer. For I tell you, I will not eat it again until it finds fulfillment in the kingdom of God.'
>
> After taking the cup, he gave thanks and said, 'Take this and divide it among you. For I tell you I will not drink again from the fruit of the vine until the kingdom of God comes.'
>
> And he took bread, gave thanks and broke it, and gave it to them, saying, 'This is my body given for you; do this in remembrance of me.'
>
> In the same way, after the supper he took the cup,

> saying, 'This cup is the new covenant in my blood, which is poured out for you. But the hand of him who is going to betray me is with mine on the table. The Son of Man will go as it has been decreed. But woe to that man who betrays him!" Luke 22:14-22

There are powerful truths throughout these verses, but for now we're going to focus on the last one: woe to him who betrays. Jesus, of course, knew that the "woeful" one sat in our midst.

Can you picture it? If I were Jesus (which thankfully I'm not), I probably would have whispered to John, the disciple nearest Him, and said, "please pass this down but skip Judas since he doesn't deserve it."

Wouldn't it be comfortable to stop here? To think of Jesus' great gift that was given to the very one who would betray Him?

Oh, wait. That includes me. Probably you, too. I doubt we've accepted a bag of coins to hurt Jesus. Actually, I'm not sure that statement is even true, for I know there have been times when I don't let my light shine as bright for fear of offending others. If I'm gut-level honest, I wouldn't be surprised if there have been times when I kept my faith a secret knowing that divulging it might cost me.

Other times the betrayal comes in a different form, a checking of whose company I'm in before saying certain things (either letting the Christianese flow around my devout friends or the exact opposite around those who aren't).

Whatever the case, Judas makes us look good if we're hoping to rank against another, but when we stop and make the comparison to Christ and Christ alone, our perspective has to change as we see that Easter and the Last Supper represent a gift to the underserving—and we are they!

PAUSE AND REFLECT

1. Has there been a time when you weren't sure if you would give something to a certain person because you felt like they wouldn't appreciate it? If so, what did you do?

2. Have there been times when you received a gift and it became apparent that you didn't appreciate it as much as the giver had hoped?

3. This isn't meant as a chance to start beating yourself up, but I hope you recognize that you and me are part of the undeserving. If you accept this reality, stop and thank Jesus for a gift freely given even though you

didn't deserve it. If you don't believe you're underserving of it, ask Jesus to gently reveal ways to you that you "fall short of the glory of God" (Romans 3:23).

DAY 14. ARGUING GREATNESS

Jesus had just finished breaking bread and sharing wine, serving what we would come to know as The Last Supper. Then He spoke of one who would betray Him. Questions arose as the disciples wondered who could do such a thing. My guess is they tried cracking the mystery by highlighting their own strengths while emphasizing others' weaknesses.

It is mere speculation, but whatever they said caused an argument "among them as to which of them was considered to be greatest" (Luke 22:24).

It's incomprehensible how quickly the conversation changed:

> "The Son of Man will go as it has been decreed. But woe to that man who betrays him' They began to question among themselves which of them it might be who would do this.

A dispute also arose among them as to which of them was considered to be greatest." Luke 22:22-24

Can you see the absolute disconnect? These men sat with Jesus, heard his alarming statements, yet they dared debate who at the table was the greatest, as if there was any contest. It's like sitting in the Oval Office and telling the President you wield more power than him.

I would love to believe Jesus was so distraught with what He knew was about to come that He missed out on the whole "I'm better than you" conflict; that He heard their murmurings without ever really processing what they said.

Easter highlights our humanity and Jesus' deity.

Truth be told, I want to convince myself that Jesus missed or overlooked it because if He did He might not pay much attention to the times when I argue my own greatness. Ironically, I also swing to the other side of the pendulum and contend that I'm not good enough for Jesus to care about, let alone save, that I have to reach a certain level before qualifying to be in His presence. Regardless of where I fall on that spectrum on any given day, I attempt to believe Jesus missed their quarrel—and mine.

But I can't. Jesus spoke directly to their claims:

> "The greatest among you should be like the youngest, and the one who rules like the one who serves. For who is greater, the one who is at the table or the one who serves? Is it not the one who is at the table? But I am among you as one who serves." Luke 22:26b-27

I can't help but look at Jesus through my lens of humanity. If I were in His shoes (a much too ridiculous statement if ever there was one), I'd say, "Forget this! If these are the guys I've poured into for the last three years and *they* still bicker over petty things, then what's the point? I'm not about to let others beat and devastate my body for *them!*"

Fortunately for all of us, I am not He and better still, He's not me. In fact, just this one incident points to one overwhelming fact: Easter highlights our humanity and Jesus' deity.

Have you ever seen the picture in religious tracts that depicts the great chasm of sin between God and us? The gap is so large we can't span it on our own, so the next image shows the cross as a bridge between the two. It's an amazing illustration of the work of the cross, yet somehow it's given me license to skip across that divide and act as if it was a mere stream rather than a raging river. As I reflect upon the events leading up to the cross, I realize the span between Jesus and the rest of us is beyond measure.

If I'm lucky, I'll pause at that great divide, recognize whose presence I'm in and will stop arguing my greatness.

PAUSE AND REFLECT

1. Have you ever tried to cross a river that didn't have a bridge? If so, what did you do? Did you make it across?

2. Do you argue your greatness to God or question His? I do it all the time. I bet you do, too. One way I do this is by saying, "God, if you really are in charge of the universe, then you would _______." Other times I argue His greatness by thinking I know what is best for my life and getting mad at Him when He doesn't respond the way I hoped.

How about you? What are some of the ways you might argue your greatness to the Almighty? Would you dare stop, even just for a day?

3. It might seem ironic that Jesus' disciples stood in the presence of Jesus, but fought over who was the greatest. If that looks ridiculous, then how do we appear as we're filled with the Holy Spirit, yet fight to be number one?

DAY 15. PRE-SIFTING PRAYERS

Some people are germaphobes. Me? I'm a Job-aphobe. I'm not talking about the 9-5 grind. Rather, this fear comes from the guy in the Old Testament.

In the Book of Job we get a behind-the-scenes peek at Satan asking God for permission to test Job. The quick summary is that God consented and Job lost nearly everything, including his children, servants, livestock, and the support of his wife and friends.

After all this, Satan stands before God yet again, this time claiming that the only reason Job had not cursed God was because he still had his health. Listen in on this mind-blowing conversation:

> "Does Job fear God for nothing?' Satan replied. 'Have you not put a hedge around him and his household and everything he has? You have blessed the work of his hands, so that his flocks and herd are spread through the land. But stretch

> out your hand and strike everything he has, and he will surely curse you to your face.'
>
> The Lord said to Satan, 'Very well, then, everything he has is in your hands, but on the man himself do not lay a finger." Job 1:9-12a

Skip ahead a few lines and we see Job scratching painful sores with a piece of broken pottery. It's no wonder sweat drips down my forehead whenever someone mentions the name "Job."

It comes as no surprise that when I read Luke's account of Jesus' dialogue changing from serving others (Jesus' rebuttal to their arguments of greatness) to saying to Peter (who was also known as Simon), "Simon, Simon, Satan has asked to sift you as wheat" (Luke 22:31), I start wiggling in my seat, anxious to skip to the next section. It sounds too similar to the disturbing words found in Job. The only difference is that this time we don't get an in-depth look at the conversation between God and Satan. Instead Jesus says, "Simon, Simon, Satan has asked to sift you as wheat. But I have prayed for you, Simon, that your faith may not fail. And when you have turned back, strengthen your brothers" (Luke 22:31-32).

My mind sees Simon Peter declaring he'll stand by Jesus, come what may. But Jesus knew the "sifting" would happen and that Peter, for one regrettable moment, would deny even knowing Jesus. In doing so,

I gloss over something more remarkable than my mind can comprehend: Jesus prayed for Simon Peter.

Don't you dare skip over it too! Soak it in as I repeat it again for you and me: Jesus prayed for Simon.

I have a friend who is going through incredible hardships. No, let me correct that. There are many of us that have been walking through trials, but this particular friend created a Facebook group to pray for her and her ministry. One of her posts went beyond asking us to pray: "and if you don't mind," she concluded, "would you write out part of your prayer for me, please?" Weakened in the battle, she didn't just want prayers, she wanted to hear our words and let them bring her to the very throne of God.

Unlike the prayers for my friend, we aren't privy to the exact words of Jesus's prayer for Peter. Instead we get a brief glimpse of the talk between Jesus and God:

> "But I have prayed for you, Simon, that your faith may not fail. And when you have turned back, strengthen your brothers." Luke 22:32-33

Friend, I don't know if you're in the midst of a trial, but I can guarantee that if you aren't, you will be at some point in your future. It's just inevitable. But here's a glorious beauty we can hang on to: before Satan could test Simon Peter's faith, Jesus Himself prayed for him.

Chances are He does the same for you and me.

PAUSE AND REFLECT

1. Are you a germaphobe? What about a Job-aphobe? Are there parts of Job's story that scare you, and if so, which?

2. What if you were Simon and heard that Jesus prayed for you? Do you believe that Jesus might pray on your behalf?

3. Romans 8:26-27 says, "In the same way, the Spirit helps us in our weakness. We do not know what we ought to pray for, but the Spirit himself intercedes for us through wordless groans. And he who searches our hearts knows the mind of the Spirit, because the Spirit intercedes for God's people in accordance with the will of God." How does it impact you knowing that the Holy Spirit intercedes to God on your behalf?

DAY 16. THE CUSTOM OF THE WILL

My Girlie and I love to laugh and giggle. Sure, I don't see her as much now as I did just a few years back before the teen years propelled her into her room for hours at a time. I'm no competition for face timing with friends or sleeping in. But the time we do share is usually fun as we talk about our days. I know I only have a few years left before she leaves for college and that our relationship will change then. I probably won't see her on a daily basis and the number of times we talk each day will diminish, but I'm banking on the fact that the foundation we've established thus far will cause us to keep current with each other, even when we can't see each other face to face.

Perhaps it's that same kind of foundation we see in Luke 22:39 as "Jesus went out as usual to the Mount of Olives, and his disciples followed him." In the absence of being side-by-side with His Father, Jesus made it His habit to go somewhere secluded to connect with Him.

Part of me loves that Judas told the high priests exactly where they could find Jesus for he knew that

Jesus "often withdrew to lonely places and prayed" (Luke 5:16).

We know the events leading up to the crucifixion did not surprise Jesus. He wasn't shocked by His arrest or the trials since He was fully aware of what was about to happen to Him. And yet, even with that knowledge, He still carved out time to go and pray, as was His custom. Actually, "even with that knowledge" isn't the right way to say it." "Because of that knowledge" is more fitting. Knowing what was about to come fueled His need even more to go and pray.

Why?

Let's listen in to His words:

> "Jesus went out as usual to the Mount of Olives, and his disciples followed him. On reaching the place, he said to them, 'Pray that you will not fall into temptation.' He withdrew about a stone's throw beyond them, knelt down and prayed, **"Father, if you are willing, take this cup from me; yet not my will, but yours be done."** Luke 22:39-42, emphasis mine

The urge for self to take control loomed nearby, the desire for safety and protection threatening to win over the upcoming physical and emotional pain.

We know it was Jesus' habit to retire to the Mount of Olives to pray, but we don't always know the specifics about what He prayed. Even without that knowledge, Luke 22:39-42 offers an incredible lesson in prayer:

"Not my will, but yours be done."

I want to be known as a woman who prays, as is her custom. I want God to know me as a woman who desires to do His will, even at the cost of my own.

I hope you'll join me in developing the custom of the will.

PAUSE AND REFLECT

1. What are a few things you are known for that another would say you do "as is your custom?"

2. What does your prayer life look like, especially when things are more challenging? Do you find yourself at your Mount of Olives praying more than before, or are you more likely to run to a valley and isolate yourself from prayer?

3. My guess is many of us need to hit the pause button and pray "not my will, but yours." I encourage you to take time to do so today. Perhaps it's a family matter you need to give God control over again, or maybe it's

your finances or how you spend your free time. Whatever the case, let's develop the custom of the will.

DAY 17. THE AGONY OF BETRAYAL

11:46 am, August 22nd. That's when every suspicion I tried keeping my mind from believing became too obvious to ignore. *She* existed. "'Til death do us part" soured as my husband's actions proved those words meant something different to him than they did to me.

I ended the call that verified all suspicions and collapsed to the cold tile floor. Anguish suddenly rippled through every part of my being in ways I never could have imagined. I felt like I was being swallowed whole by a dark, thick mire and I feared I wouldn't survive. If it weren't for God's grace and provision, I probably wouldn't have.

Betrayal cuts to the core in ways that very few things can. It isn't like the waves of excruciating pain of a broken bone that shoot out from the injured area but eventually subsides with proper treatment. Nor is it like the quick flash of anger that darts across our face after a friend accidentally says something hurtful—and apologizes a breath after the words leave her mouth.

No, this pain pierces to the marrow, an unquenchable grief that only comes from knowing the betraying act was committed by someone who claimed to love or care for us. It's pain that is amplified by the stark reality Michael Card summed up so well: "Only a friend can betray a friend. A stranger has nothing to gain."

No friend or loved one would do such a thing, or so we once believed.

And then it drops. Ends. Destroys.

Jesus knew the kiss of betrayal, the lips that dared to brush His cheek as a signal to others that He was the one to take away. It was the original kiss of death.

> "Friend, do what you are here to do." Matthew 26:50

Don't gloss this over. It might seem to pale when compared to the crucifixion, but don't let the knowledge of what happened next diminish the ache of that moment.

The ache . . . . and the beauty.

> Jesus received the first kiss of death.

How can I say that? Because deep within Judas' inconceivable act, betraying the one he had spent virtually every moment with for the past three years, the man who called him friend and disciple, we see something even more unthinkable: Jesus still did it! He knew full well what was going to happen, He could have prevented it, made sure He never encountered Judas, never poured His truth into him. But he didn't stop it and therein lies the most awe-inspiring truth: the cross is for all. We diminish the lavishness of the sacrifice if we reduce it to something given only to those deserving it. It started with the one who betrayed Him, and ends there as well, for the One who knew what Judas would do also knows what you and I are capable of.

He knew fully, yet it wasn't enough to stop Him because love trumped all.

And it continues to do so.

PAUSE AND REFLECT

1. Think about a time in which a friend or family member betrayed you. How did you feel? How long did it take to get over that hurt (assuming you have, which doesn't always happen)?

2. Do you believe that love trumps all?

3. If you said yes to the question above, how does that change any belief you might have that you must earn your salvation or that you're unworthy of Jesus' great

sacrifice? I've heard it said that one of Satan's greatest tools is to convince us we aren't worthy of Christ's love and are, therefore, ineligible to receive it. It is partially true; we are wholly and fully undeserving of what He gave us on the cross, yet despite our infinite lack, or perhaps better said, *because* of our infinite lack, Jesus extends it to us. What will you do today to let love trump all?

DAY 18. FALLING GLORY

The pull of gravity is stronger in my house than anywhere else. I'm certain of it. Why else would my daughter and I constantly crash into one another and trip over chair legs?

I jest, of course, to rationalize our clumsiness, but there actually was a time when the pull of gravity was stronger than normal. Read the following account of a strange incident in which everyone dropped to the ground:

> "So Judas, having procured a band of soldiers and some officers from the chief priests and the Pharisees, went there with lanterns and torches and weapons. Then Jesus, knowing all that would happen to him, came forward and said to them, 'Whom do you seek?' They answered him, 'Jesus of Nazareth.' Jesus said to them, 'I am he.' Judas, who betrayed him, was standing with them. When

> Jesus said to them, 'I am he,' **they drew back and fell to the ground.** So he asked them again, 'Whom do you seek?' And they said, 'Jesus of Nazareth.'" John 18:3-7, emphasis mine

Picture 300-600 Roman soldiers coming to arrest Jesus. They know their mission: arrest Jesus. And yet, as they go to do so, they all drop to the ground.

I once heard it taught that the soldiers were overwhelmed in the presence of Jesus and were showing a moment of reverence to Him. It seems odd to assume that hundreds of people intent on arresting Him simultaneously decided to show Him reverence. How can this be justified based on what they would do to Him later?

Could it really be just a sudden pull of gravity that knocked them from their feet?

Let's look at the verses again for a subtle clue. Pay close attention to the question the soldiers and officials asked and Jesus' response:

> "Jesus, knowing all that was going to happen to him, went out and asked them, 'Who is it you want?'
>
> 'Jesus of Nazareth,' they replied.
>
> 'I am he,' Jesus said. (And Judas the traitor was standing there with them.) When Jesus said, 'I am

> he,' they drew back and fell to the ground." John 18:4-6

They went looking for a man with a common name from a small village, but rather than answering with a small name, Jesus identified Himself in the same way God did with Moses from the burning bush:

I AM.

When originally said, God was instructing the stammering and fearful Moses to return to Egypt and ask Pharaoh to release the Israelites. He commanded Moses to return to the place where Moses was known to be a murderer and didn't fit in with either the royalty or the enslaved people of his ancestry. Riddled with doubts and concerns, Moses prodded over and over until the *ego* came out, the *ego eimi*, that is, which are the Greek words meaning I AM (note: the following is from the Old Testament and therefore would have been said in Hebrew).

> "Moses said to God, 'Suppose I go to the Israelites and say to them, 'The God of your fathers has sent me to you,' and they ask me, 'What is his name?' Then what shall I tell them?
>
> God said to Moses, 'I am who I am. This is what you are to say to the Israelites: I am has sent me to you.'" Exodus 3:13-14

We see *ego eimi* again in John 8:58 when Jesus said, "Verily, verily, I say unto you, before Abraham was, I am." Since *ego eimi* is translated here simply as "I am," many theologians contend that the best translation for John 18:6 is, "When Jesus said, 'I am,' they drew back and fell to the ground." John 18:6

Did you catch that? I am. Period. Not I am a strong person, or I am a chocoholic, or I am God. Just two simple words. Only when spoken by God or Jesus do they form a complete sentence, a sentence that packs a punch. Literally as hundreds of grown men collapsed to the ground, all at the name of I AM.

PAUSE AND REFLECT

1. We serve a mighty God. No, I mean a *mighty* God. I'm too quick to diminish the power of the One many of us have committed our lives to. Let's stop and reflect upon the incredible power of God—a power that can literally push hundreds to the ground at just the mention of His name.

2. Does the realization that Jesus saying I AM is enough to knock hundreds to the ground impact your view of Him? Does it challenge the way you pray, which really is just a form of coming to Jesus and talking to Him?

3. If you have a personal relationship with I AM, stop and thank Him for His redeeming power in your life.

DAY 19. WHEN LOVE TRUMPS JUSTICE

We can barely make it through a week without hearing accusations of unwarranted police brutality or teachers in a position of trust being arrested for having sex with a minor. These are but a few examples where someone wrongfully uses their authority. If we look at the various stages of Jesus' arraignment, we'll see the same abuse unfold time and again. Let's focus on the following example:

> "Meanwhile, the high priest questioned Jesus about his disciples and his teaching.
>
> 'I have spoken openly to the world,' Jesus replied. 'I always taught in synagogues or at the temple, where all the Jews come together. I said nothing in secret. Why question me? Ask those who heard me. Surely they know what I said.'

> When Jesus said this, **one of the officials nearby struck him in the face.** 'Is this the way you answer the high priest?' he demanded." John 18:19-22, emphasis mine

The official did not have the authority to strike anyone. Jesus had not yet been deemed innocent or guilty. Put those two facts together and it should have been an outrage that Annas hit Jesus while He was on trial.

We could cry of the injustice. In fact, we should. You see, that is the very point of the crucifixion, an issue that is so hard to comprehend that sometimes it helps to focus on one of the most minute details.

If one of my kids came home from school and said someone slapped them, I'd be on the phone with their educators before they could finish telling me what happened. But as we know, there weren't phones then and the line of people standing up to defend Jesus was in short supply.

As unfair as it was for someone to slap Jesus merely for His accurate response, it is equally unthinkable that Jesus would later be condemned for something He didn't do. No, scratch that. The weight of our sins by far surpassed a blow to the face.

It isn't logical that we are deemed clean because of something an innocent man did on our behalf. It wasn't fair that an innocent man should die for something He didn't do, but the cross isn't about justice. Instead, it was the way in which love trumped justice.

PAUSE AND REFLECT

1. How do you feel when you see someone hurting an innocent person?

2. What would you do if someone dear to you was intentionally hurt for something that was no fault of their own?

3. How would you respond if you did something that merited a painful, excruciating consequence, yet someone who loved you chose to accept the penalty for you?

DAY 20. COLD SEEPS IN, HUMANITY FLOWS OUT

My mom was in marching band. Dad was too. So was my big sis. Guess what I did when I started high school?

You're close, but not quite. I had to be slightly rebellious, so I joined the color guard and twirled flags while the band played. Nevertheless, I was still out there with the band during every practice, which somehow always happened to go until 9pm four nights a week. In Colorado. In the winter.

My feet didn't care for that combination, especially as they marched through snow in tennis shoes. Before long, a pain settled in every night, intense pangs shooting through my feet. The only way to make them subside was to smack my legs as hard as I could against the mattress. I found relief for a few brief seconds, then repeated the process. It was quite the awkward—and painful!—way to try falling asleep.

The family legacy of marching band in high school ended with my sister. I completed the season then traded in the flag for more books.

I didn't have to convince anyone of my decision since my family encouraged me to do whatever I could to help alleviate my pain.

Even if you've can't sympathize with thumping your feet against your bed because of nerve pain, I'm sure you can relate to the desire to avoid pain.

For me this includes physical as well as emotional pain, which is why I want to skip over parts of the Easter story. I race through the last chapters of the gospels, pretending to be anxious for the exhilarating ending, but really just wanting to minimize the parts that hurt (which ironically are pretty much the entire Easter story).

It is more than my mind can comprehend: chunks of flesh ripped off my Savior's body as the cat-o-nine tails tore into His flesh while people who once chanted "Hosanna" changed their shouts to "Crucify!"

I'll never fully comprehend the pain Jesus endured on my behalf, but I can take baby steps. For example, I can make myself remember the pain I felt from being cold and then I'll have a .00008% better understanding of what Jesus felt.

Mark 14:54 says, "Peter followed him at a distance, right into the courtyard of the high priest. There he sat with the guards and **warmed himself at the fire**" (emphasis, mine).

Peter got to warm himself by the fire, but what about Jesus? Was He cold? The trials happened throughout the night, the portion of the day when it is coldest. I know it's like saying that the first day of kindergarten is as hard as defending a dissertation. My comparison is painfully weak, yet it starts me down the road to recognizing that Jesus wasn't just God incarnate, but He was also human and suffered from the elements as well.

So human, in fact, that as Peter warmed himself and Jesus didn't, the coldness seeped in while humanity flowed out.

PAUSE AND REFLECT

1. If your health can handle it, willingly subject yourself to an extreme temperature today. Depending on where you live, you might go outside early in the morning, sit and read a book in the blazing sun, or hold your hand in a glass of ice-cold water for a minute. Think about how it makes you feel.

2. Think about a time you got hurt physically. Maybe it was a large-scale hurt, or perhaps it was something small. How did it feel? Did it impact other parts of your life or hinder you from doing the things you normally do?

3. Now think about the event that caused you the most physical pain. How does that compare to what Christ endured?

DAY 21. SEARCHING FOR THE OBVIOUS

Many years ago, not long after my sister got her driver's license, Mom asked us to run a few errands. The first item checked off the list, we headed to the next store to purchase a battery. We found the one we needed, paid, and returned to the parking lot where my sister began fumbling through her purse in search of her keys.

"I know I put them in here," she said confidently, but as the seconds turned to minutes, certainty waned. We returned to the store, hoping my sister left them near the register, but they weren't there. We asked the clerk if he had seen them and began searching the store after he said no.

Kim and I walked back to the parking lot, our search becoming more desperate. We walked the perimeter of the car checking the ground and peered into windows.

“Maybe I dropped them and they fell under the car,” my sister said. She got on her hands and knees and sure enough, she found them. But the keys weren’t under the car. When Kim put her hand on the pavement, she felt the pressure in her palm and realized the very thing we were looking for had been in her hand the whole time.

I don’t tell this story to make fun of my sister, for most of us have done the same kind of thing at one time or another (I’m the type to frantically search for my sunglasses while they’re perched on my head). I’m sharing her experience because I think we all look high and low for something that is right in front of us. We even find it in the Easter story.

Caiaphas was the highest ranking priest in Jesus’ day. You would think that someone who had spent nearly two decades helping others search for and follow God would be ecstatic about the arrival of a man who claimed to be the Son of God—the promised Messiah--*and* performed miracles that proved His claim. However, as we know, that was not his response.

> “The high priest said to him, ‘I charge you under oath by the living God: Tell us if you are the Messiah, the Son of God.’

'You have said so,' Jesus replied. 'But I say to all of you: From now on you will see the Son of Man sitting at the right hand of the Mighty One and coming on the clouds of heaven.'

Then the high priest tore his clothes and he said, 'He has spoken blasphemy! Why do we need any more witnesses? Look, now you have heard the blasphemy. What do you think?'

'He is worthy of death,' they answered.

Then they spit in his face and struck him with their fists." Matthew 26:63b-66

The very One Caiaphas had been waiting for stood before him. He could have dropped to the ground worshipping and accepting Jesus, but instead he became incensed by the audacity of someone who claimed such a position and, therefore, kept searching for what was in front of him. Before we can blame him and pass him off as a miner who mistook a large nugget for fool's gold, we have to remember some of the things he undoubtedly knew full well, commands given to his ancestors as they made their way into the Promised Land.

"If you hear it said about one of the towns the Lord your God is giving you to live in that

> troublemakers have arisen among you and have led the people of their town astray, saying, 'Let us go and worship other gods' (gods you have not known), then you must inquire, probe and investigate it thoroughly. And if it is true and it has been proved that this detestable thing has been done among you, you must certainly put to the sword all who live in that town. You must destroy it completely, both its people and its livestock. You are to gather all the plunder of the town into the middle of the public square and completely burn the town and all its plunder as a whole burnt offering to the Lord your God." Deuteronomy 13:13-14

Undoubtedly, the high priest knew full well that if something arose that would cause people to drift towards other gods, then it must be destroyed. In his fervor to remain committed to what the *Law of God* said, Caiaphas missed the *Son of God.*

Just like my sister could only find her keys once she lowered herself to the ground, we too run the risk of missing the enormity of Easter unless we lay down our pride (and ourselves) and stop to look at the very thing right in front of us.

PAUSE AND REFLECT

1. Have you ever searched for something that was right in front of you?

2. If you go to an Easter egg hunt this year, watch the enthusiasm of the kids as they dash off trying to find as many eggs as possible. Observe their persistence and excitement. Does the effort you put into searching for Christ—whether that means getting to know Him for the first time or letting that relationship run deeper even after the years you have known Him—rival the energy and persistence kids put into their searching?

3. Regardless of what scriptures Caiaphas might have used to justify his decision, the fact remains that he stood in the presence of holiness and condemned it. Have you ever been there? Perhaps someone needed a listening ear, but instead you rushed off to another meeting, or maybe they needed sympathy, and instead you weighed them down with your opinions and judgments. If you fall in that category with me, might I offer us this prayer:

Jesus, I miss you. I keep overlooking you. I get so busy and preoccupied with my own things, worrying about what might happen next or trying to figure out what to do. In the process, I overlook those you place in front of me and neglect this incredible gift you give me called today. Teach me, Lord. Teach me to see you in the beautiful as well as in the mundane. Help me to look for you in the fun, as well as in the trying. Forgive me for overlooking you.
Amen.

DAY 22. PERISHING BILLIONS

We mine for it and search for it if we misplace it. Gold is exquisite and adds beauty and value to most anything. Maybe that is why Solomon chose to use so much of it when building the temple.

"Solomon covered the inside of the temple with pure gold" (I Kings 6:21) and "he also covered the floors of both the inner and outer rooms of the temple with gold" (I Kings 6:30).

Can you imagine that? How would you feel standing inside a 90 foot long building that is covered in gold?

This makes me think back to a time when I was working in Juarez, Mexico. After a week of playing soccer in the hot sun and with no running water, we were quite the sight (and smell) to behold. A colleague and I had just crossed the border into El Paso when our truck broke down. The closest place to call for help was a five-star hotel. When I took one step inside and saw the beautiful and immaculate marble floors, I froze in place, knowing I was too filthy to enter.

That's how I think I'd feel standing inside a building filled with God's presence, designed to give Him glory, especially one that was covered in 8.1 million pounds of gold.

Place yourself there for a minute. Try to grasp the beauty and grandeur of it, like the ultimate jewelry store on steroids, all to proclaim the might and glory of our God.

Now imagine being one of the people who was accustomed to entering the temple on a regular basis, aware of its glimmering splendor. What would you do if someone said it would be destroyed or, even more remarkably, that they would rebuild it in a mere three days?

These were the charges held against Jesus.

> "The chief priests and the whole Sanhedrin were looking for false evidence against Jesus so that they could put him to death. But they did not find any, though many false witnesses came forward.
>
> Finally two came forward and declared, "This fellow said, 'I am able to destroy the temple of God and rebuild it in three days.'" Matthew 26:59-61

Of course, they didn't understand what we know now: that Jesus was referring to His body. Without that insight, his claim was radical and far-fetched, just like another that is equally true, but few of us embrace: those 8.1 million pounds of gold were nothing more than rubbish. It's hard to believe, but pay attention to what 1 Peter 1:18-19 says:

> "For you know that it was not with perishable things such as silver or gold that you were redeemed from the empty way of life handed down to you from your ancestors, but with the precious blood of Christ, a lamb without blemish or defect."

Did you catch that? Gold, even the vast quantities found in Solomon's Temple, is referred to as perishable when compared to the immeasurable value of the precious blood of Christ.

PAUSE AND REFLECT

1. What is one of the most valuable things you own? What would you do if you lost it? Would you search for it at great length?

2. Think again about one of your most valuable possessions. How would you describe it? Would rubbish be one of the adjectives you use?

3. Solomon's Temple, valued at $216 billion just for the silver and gold, is rubbish when compared to something even more precious: the blood of Christ. How does it make you feel that something so valuable was given for your benefit?

DAY 23: THE HALF MUSKETEER

"All for one and one for all, united we stand divided we fall."

Those are the words musketeers would chant, at least *full* musketeers. Jesus, however, was the original *half* musketeer. One for all.

Caiaphas, the high priest that year, said it best, although he could not have known how fitting his words would be: "You do not realize that it is better for you that one man die for the people than that the whole nation perish" (John 11:50).

Caiaphas had no idea that his words were prophetic. He uttered them shortly after Jesus raised Lazarus from the dead. John 11 tells us that after seeing what Jesus did, many Jews put their faith in Jesus. Some of those new believers went to the Pharisees and recounted what Jesus had done. Rather than sharing in their joy, the chief priests and the Pharisees called a meeting of the Sanhedrin.

Isn't it interesting that once Jesus did something that no one else had ever done before, some believed, while others convened to devise a plan to destroy Him? Even more astonishing, the Bible Exposition Commentary says, "the high priest, Caiaphas, was a Sadducee, not a Pharisee; but the two factions could always get together to fight a common enemy." Who was the enemy and what was the potential threat?

> "'What are we accomplishing?' they asked. 'Here is this man performing many miraculous signs. If we let him go on like this, everyone will believe in him, and then the Romans will come and take away both our place and our nation.'" John 11:47-48

It was then that Caiaphas said,

> "You know nothing at all! You do not realize that it is better for you that one man die for the people than that the whole nation perish." John 11:49-50

Even though he was the high priest, Caiaphas made his proclamation as a self-protecting measure rather than prophecy, but prophetic it was. Days later, Jesus would in fact die, not to save only the small nation in which He lived, but all who stated their belief in Him.

Through the high priest's announcement and subsequent actions, the original half musketeer's chant can more accurately be said as:

None for one,
But one for all.

By His blood we live,
Without it we fall.

PAUSE AND REFLECT

1. Think back to when you were in school. Was there a time when someone did something they shouldn't have, but the teacher didn't know who it was? Did the teacher threaten to punish the whole class unless someone confessed? If so, would you have told on the person to avoid incurring a consequence for something you didn't do?

2. Continuing from the first question, would you have taken the punishment, even if you were innocent, just to prevent the rest of the class from receiving it too? If yes, that would mean that you would have to pay the price for someone's actions, while the person who did the wrong would leave the classroom without any form of punishment. Could you do it?

3. Our sins extend far beyond shooting a spit wad when the teacher isn't looking, yet Jesus still took them on Himself—one for all. Let's stop for a few moments to thank Him for what He did.

DAY 24. THE DISCIPLINE OF SILENCE

I wish I could say I'm quick to ponder an event, chewing on its impact before sharing it with others. But, no. As soon as I hang up the phone after receiving good news, I hit speed dial to share it with someone else. If the news is bad my tendency is to call several people or start a group text.

So when one of my spiritual mentors talked to me about the discipline of silence, I was stunned. Sure, I'm aware of fasting and the other disciplines she mentioned, but silence? I didn't even have a reference point to understand that one.

Seeing the confused look on my face, she went on to explain. "The discipline of silence can also be called the discipline of secrecy. It is doing something without telling anyone other than God. Rather than broadcasting a request, keep something troubling you tucked between you and God and wait to see how He responds."

The concept amazes me. Within a few days I had the perfect opportunity to try it out. I'm writing this just a few weeks afterwards, so I'm still in the middle of the silence. In other words, I'm purposefully not sharing any of the details, but instead will say that it was an event that would normally shake me deep. It affected me, and my kids, who are at those blessed ages when they usually focus only on their own worlds, repeatedly asked each other "what in the world happened to Mom?" Eventually they asked me, "Mom, what can we do for you?"

Instead of answering them and sharing it with my tribe, I've silently taken it before God. Okay, I confess that at first I wasn't so silent. In fact, I was rather loud as I shook my fist before the heavenlies asking, "God, can you believe…?" But as the days turn to weeks, I find myself forgetting the incident more and more, no longer waiting for a final ruling on how this might affect me. I put my case before the One whose judgment is even more secure than the highest court and I have found rest.

It has been amazing, and apparently I'm not the only one to feel this way. Watch this quiet interaction:

> "When he was accused by the chief priests and the elders, he gave no answer. Then Pilate asked him, 'Don't you hear the testimony they are bringing against you?' But Jesus made no reply, not even to a single charge—to the great amazement of the governor." Mathew 27:12-14

Do you know what I hear in His silence? Trust. Sheer, unadulterated trust.

Jesus stood before someone with the authority to clear His name and release Him. He could have launched into a powerful defense or turned the tables of accusation by pointing at the ones who plotted His arrest.

But He didn't.

Why?

Because He knew His whole purpose for being on earth was to save us and He could only do that by sacrificing His life. But even beyond that, He knew His Father's plan was good—good for us, good for the world, good for forever—even though it would be excruciating in the present.

And so, with faith ringing louder than words, He remained perfectly silent.

PAUSE AND REFLECT

1. Have you ever had accusations launched against you? How did you respond? Think about both your verbal response (the things you actually said) as well as your hypothetical response (the things you later said, "Oh, I should have said . . ."). Reflect on the ways it impacted you and how long you mentally dwelt on it (days, weeks, months or, gulp—even longer).

2. Are you a broadcaster or a quiet muller?

3. Regardless of your answer above, we have a great challenge. For my fellow broadcasters, ask God to stretch your trust by committing to practice the discipline of silence with the next 'ugh' that comes your way. When tempted to bemoan the event to others, let it serve as a reminder to lay it before the One who laid everything down for you and me.

To you quiet muller-folks, rather than simply dwelling on an event (dare I say brewing?), redirect the quiet. Rather than chewing on it alone, expand your trust by telling someone who cares. No, we aren't practicing the discipline of silence by talking to a friend! Share it with God. Tell Him how it impacts you, what fears it causes, or whatever might be the case. And then commit to wait silently to see how He moves.

DAY 25. THE MARROW OF THE MATTER

"Quick. Sign me up before I change my mind. This scares the tar out of me," I said as I signed up to be a potential bone marrow donor. It wasn't on my radar, but when a group of volunteers at an outdoor performance reached out and encouraged people to sign up, I did.

I thought of my dear friend Kate who has battled cancer for years, and another friend who nearly died when doctors aggressively tried to kill the very thing that was ravaging her body.

Bone marrow transplants would not help either of these sweet souls, but their constant eagerness to press on and fight for their lives reminds me that I have something neither of them currently do: excellent health and an ability to help someone who doesn't.

So I put my name on the list, secretly hoping they were just taking names without knowing if I would be a good match for someone who needed what I could give. But no. They came prepared.

"If you'll just swab the inside of your cheeks for me, we'll be able to know your blood type and everything else needed to determine if you're a good match for someone on the registry."

I swabbed and sweated. I've had bad experiences the few times I tried to give blood, my rolling and collapsing veins making the attempts to draw it both painful and futile as my blood stopped flowing before they had enough. "Sorry, ma'am," the nurse said to this chicken-hearted girl with tears streaming down her face, "but we won't be able to use your blood."

I can see my veins, those blue lines running down my arms that cause the nurses such grief, but my bone marrow is much deeper. My training in biochemistry makes me keenly aware of what is involved: that they would have to puncture a bone to withdraw the marrow that can mean life to someone else.

It freaks me out to no end to think of having a needle inserted *through my bone.* My fear runs deep, but another reality runs deeper: someone's life might depend on it.

So why did I put my name on the list? Because my name is written in the Book of Life, and it got there only because someone loved me down to the marrow. As we venture through the pain in the days to come, we're going to want to pass over the anguish and sorrow. Please don't. Trust me, I know how tempting it is to overlook pain I can't wrap my head around, but if we skip that, we run the risk of not understanding that marrow-deep love that is ours for the taking.

PAUSE AND REFLECT

1. How do you feel about needles?

2. What causes you the most pain? Would you voluntarily subject yourself to that for the sake of someone else?

3. We're tempted to skip the painful, but Jesus willingly signed up for it. Think about any circumstance you said you would avoid, even if it benefited someone else. How does that compare to:

- Being flogged with broken glass or shards of bone?
- Having thorns pressed deep into the brow?
- Being humiliated in front of friends and family?
- Having someone drive sharp nails into your feet and hands?

- Being too weak to support yourself to get a breath of air?
- Dying of asphyxiation?

DAY 26. LEARNING THROUGH SUFFERING

"It just isn't faaaaaaiiiiirrrr!"

As a mom of two young kids, I hear this phrase all too often, always ending with a long and drawn-out description of the supposed inequality. I'm accustomed to hearing my little ones say it, but sometimes another person in my family groans it, too: me.

We seem to be hard-wired for justice and long to know why something happened. If the answer isn't obvious, it doesn't take long for us to start banging on heaven's gates demanding an explanation.

Why, God? we shout. *Why do I have to go through this? It just isn't fair.*

I can't begin to know the thoughts of God or know His answer to the question. Instead I'll skip to something I do know about: parenthood. I'm fine with being perceived as the bad or mean mom if it will help my kids learn and grow.

For example, I constantly asked my kids to rinse their dishes before plopping them in the dishwasher, but the more I asked, the less they did. Finally I made them pull a few plates out of the dishwasher and clean off the dried-on gunk. No use. I took away dishwasher privileges and made them hand-wash their dishes on given days. Still, no apparent change.

Finally I made them pull every dish and utensil out of the dishwasher when it was brimming and ready to be run and told them to wash everything by hand. And you know what? From that night on the dishes suddenly went in much cleaner and came out without macaroni and cheese crusted onto every bowl and fork.

As a mom I wanted to make things a little uncomfortable for my kids so they would learn, for sometimes pain is the best teacher. In fact, even Jesus learned from pain. Hebrews 5:8 says, "Son though he was, he learned obedience from what he suffered."

I don't know about you, but that verse really makes my head spin and brings a halt to my excuses for disobedience. If Jesus was perfect and sinless, then why did He need to learn obedience? I don't have an answer to this question, but there is something deeper in the text that intrigues and baffles me.

We can't see it when reading the above verse in English, but there was a play on words in the original Greek text. The word we translate as learn comes from the Greek word *emathen*, while suffered is translated from *epathen.*

"*Emathen, epathen. Epathen, emathen.*" He learned, He suffered, He suffered, He learned.

Was it fair that Jesus had to suffer? Absolutely not! Did that suffering teach Jesus? I can't comprehend it since I don't know what Jesus needed to learn, but since scripture says Jesus learned from the pain, then I can't help but declare that to be true.

Since Jesus suffered—and then proceeded to learn from it—let's lay down the injustice chant whenever we're in a tough situation and instead proclaim a mindset of *emathen* and *epathen*, of letting the suffering teach and mold us.

PAUSE AND REFLECT

1. Do you believe Jesus learned obedience from what He suffered? Why or why not?

2. If you are a parent or are around young kids, do you ever intentionally let kids feel the pains of their choices so they will learn from it? Why or why not?

3. What is one of the hardest things you've ever done or one of the hardest trials you've had to face? What, if anything, did it teach you?

4. Here comes the tough one, but it's just between you and God. Are you ready to adopt a mentality of *emathen* and *epathen*, of accepting that there will be hard times in life, while asking God to use those times to teach, shape and refine you into His likeness?

DAY 27. EXPOSING THE CONCEALED

I have a tradition of going on a hike the first day my kids go back to school every year. I take time to reflect upon where I've been, where I'd like to go in the upcoming year, and set some goals along the way.

My time last year was so sweet that I became more and more excited for my day alone. The day finally arrived. As soon as I took the annual back-to-school pictures and dropped my kids off, I grabbed a few things and drove to a nearby hiking spot.

As expected, the time I had with God was incredible and I just wasn't ready to see that end, even as I watched the clouds growing dark. *Just a bit longer,* I kept telling myself. Minutes after I finally relented and turned around, the first crack of lightening streaked across the sky and thunder exploded over my head.

I began running as fast as I could on the rocky terrain, grateful to be headed downhill instead of up. Twenty minutes into my sprint, I felt optimistic that I would beat the rain. I even imagined myself doing a celebratory fist bump at my car—still miles away—showing my triumph over Mother Nature. As if noting my extreme arrogance, the drops started falling minutes later, followed by hail.

The good thing about being dumb enough to run in inclement weather is that no one was around to hear me yelping in pain as those tiny ice balls struck my arms, legs, and face.

Water streamed down the mountain making the path slippery and hiding the rocks that threatened to trip me or snap an ankle. I half ran, half skated down the mountainside. Forty minutes later I dove into the shelter of my car, soaked, beaten up, and cold.

The tank top I was wearing clung to my stomach itching every inch of skin it touched. I tried wringing it out, but found no relief. Finally, I peeled off the tank and started driving home in my sports bra, covering myself with a blanket to warm up and save myself from the stares and judgments of passersby. Turned out I didn't have to worry about anyone seeing me because the downpour was so fierce that there was limited visibility.

Let me repeat that: Downpour. Limited visibility.

All hopes of taking a quick shower before picking up my daughter disappeared. *Am I really going to pick up my daughter on her first day of middle school in drenched shorts and a sports bra?* I don't think the poor girl would ever be able to live that one down, nor would I ever want to inflict such a thing upon her. Being one of the most modestly dressed people you'll meet, I wasn't sure I could live it down.

Just the thought of the embarrassment terrified me. Why? Because we have an unspoken dress code and when we violate it—whether by our own volition, weather, or an unexpected wardrobe malfunction—embarrassment runs deep. We recall with remarkable detail the time we went to an event feeling underdressed, or the time our zipper was down for much too long (and I won't even mention the button-down dress that apparently would unbutton itself if anything rubbed against it, which I didn't realize until after I was slow dancing with the hubs at a wedding).

We avoid these wardrobe mishaps as much as possible, checking buttons and zippers before interviews or presentations, or, in my case, sewing buttonholes closed altogether to avoid any possibility of another mishap.

So who would voluntarily sign up for such a thing?

Someone on a mission. Someone with a purpose beyond him or herself. Someone who loved enough to let others see—yes, see more skin than normally exposed, but also to see the depths of a love so important and so limitless that personal modesty became irrelevant.

There is a theological debate as to whether or not Jesus was fully naked or wrapped in a loin cloth when He was crucified. Those who believe he was naked support that with the fact that humiliation was a key element in crucifixion. I have neither the depth of understanding nor the skill to answer this question when scholars more educated than me cannot come up with a definitive answer. Regardless of whether or not Jesus died with a strip of clothing on Him or none at all, the fact remains: it must have been humiliating and embarrassing. Deathly so. But this detail seems irrelevant and mundane when considering that His life would end from a lack of oxygen, not from the blush of embarrassment from having everything exposed.

The irony is too great to ignore: the One with nothing to hide allowed everything to be revealed so that the rest of us who live trying to conceal our true conditions of greed, idolatry, and self-absorption would be left with nothing to cover as He washed our sins clean.

> Christ allowed everything to be exposed so you would no longer have anything to conceal.

PAUSE AND REFLECT

1. What was your most embarrassing wardrobe malfunction?

2. Would you be willing to be fully exposed with no possible way to even place an arm or hand over your

most intimate parts if it somehow benefited someone else?

3. How does it impact you to know that Christ allowed everything to be exposed so that you would no longer have anything to conceal?

DAY 28. THE COURAGE OF A CRIMINAL

A Narrative

The day you die shouldn't be the best day of your life.

I knew my crimes would eventually catch up to me. I wish I could say that stopped me from committing them, but obviously it didn't.

At least I wouldn't die alone. Three of us hung there, three of us who would struggle to breathe until, one by one, we ceased to exist.

Or so I thought, but boy, was I wrong. In the end, nothing ceased and something entirely different began. But I'm getting ahead of myself.

People sneered and made fun of the man next to me.

"He saved others; let him save himself if he is the Christ of God, the Chosen One," they jeered (Luke 23:35).

You would think that would trigger the guy. I mean, I'd heard about Him and all the people He healed. I figured he would say something about the sheer number of people He healed or about His power, maybe even use it to save himself from this. But He remained quiet. Instead, it was only the guy on the cross furthest from me who was triggered.

No doubt, he didn't like the outcome that each of us would face as our breathing became more labored. Looking out for himself, he cried out to the One who remained silent, "Aren't you the Christ? Save yourself and us!" (Luke 23:39).

I couldn't take it. My crimes were real, things so wretched I won't even speak of them. But the person next to me? All he had done was heal others and speak about God and the truth. I couldn't remain quiet.

"Don't you fear God since you are under the same sentence? We are punished justly, for we are getting what our deeds deserve. But this man has done nothing wrong" (Luke 23:40-41).

I considered stopping there, for the thing I wanted to ask was so far-fetched it couldn't possibly happen, especially since I knew who I was and what I had done. I tried keeping it in, but I just couldn't.

Looking at the man next to me, I mustered the courage to ask the unthinkable. "Jesus, remember me when you come into your kingdom" (Luke 23:42).

I understand cause and effect. My actions merited my death, which was exactly why I found myself dying next to Jesus. Yet as I said, *I found myself next to Jesus!*

I figured He would remain quiet just as He did when those people mocked Him.

My words weren't intended as an insult, yet ultimately I suppose they were. How else could you interpret my words and my request, especially knowing the way I lived and what I did? I had no right to ask the Messiah to remember me. It would be more probable for a serial killer to be allowed to have a fine dinner with a king than for my request to be granted.

Although I wasn't expecting it, and definitely didn't deserve it, Jesus told me, "I tell you the truth, today you will be with me in paradise" (Luke 23:43).

Later that day, the very words Jesus spoke to me came true. I began a new life and entered paradise.

Like I said, the day you die shouldn't be the best day of your life.

Or perhaps it should.

PAUSE AND REFLECT

1. Put yourselves in the place of the convicted criminal that was sentenced to death next to Jesus. Can you imagine the courage it took to ask Jesus to remember him?

2. Do you think Jesus' response to the criminal's request was fair, unjust, or unexpected?

3. Is there something from your past or present that you think is too great for Jesus to forgive? What impact does the courage of the criminal or the mercy of the Messiah have on your belief that it's too large to hand over?

DAY 29. CURSED BY GOD

"You know the Bible says that anyone who dies on a tree is under God's curse," a woman said to me when she came to buy a desk I posted on Craigslist. Somehow or other, we connected immediately.

"What do you mean?" I asked.

"Deuteronomy 21 talks about God cursing anyone who is hung on a tree," she replied.

I never heard such a statement before and wasn't ready to defend or question it further in the middle of my living room with someone I met only minutes earlier. I helped her load the desk, then rushed inside and grabbed my Bible. I flipped to Deuteronomy to see if it really said what she claimed. Sure enough, it was there.

> "You must not leave his body on the tree overnight. Be sure to bury him that same day, **because anyone who is hung on a tree is under God's curse.** You must not desecrate the land the

LORD your God is giving you as an inheritance."
Deuteronomy 21:23, emphasis mine

I pulled out my concordances and powered up my Bible software, eager to refute what I feared this verse meant. Although the cross was made of wood and therefore part of a tree, Jesus didn't hang there with a rope around his neck, breaking it or causing Him to die of strangulation, right?

All of my resources proved me wrong. "Hung on a tree" wasn't limited to capital punishment involving a noose. It meant dying outside where the birds could peck and the flies would swarm.

In case you want to fight it as desperately as I did let me offer another verse:

> "**One of the criminals who hung there** hurled insults at him: "Aren't you the Messiah? Save yourself and us!" Luke 23:39, emphasis mine.

Three crosses, three men hanging, all of whom were under God's curse, Jesus included.

Jesus, the One who once sat at the right hand of God, His Father, took my shortcomings upon Himself. He gathered my fears that turn into excuses, which turn into not doing what I'm supposed to do (read clearly: sin!), my devotion to self rather than to God. He took all of that, along with the secret soul-battles of every other human being, and placed them upon Himself.

Just my stuff alone is enough to make God turn his head. Oh, don't stop reading! I know this is hard to grapple with, but it holds freedom too. My stuff—yours too—is so filthy that God had but one choice.

God turned His head, turned His back, and let the curse fall.

But here's what is radical and incomprehensible. He didn't turn His back on you or me. Nope. He cursed His son, turned aside, and let Him die on a tree.

Oh how I long to fast-forward, even if for a moment, to celebrate the result of this curse Jesus suffered and peek into an empty tomb. Resist this temptation with me, for the greatest parts of Easter are the unfinished aspects of it, the "in-process-ness."

Without a fancy ending or a shiny bow to wrap it up, stand with me for a moment in despondent humility at the foot of the cross. Gaze upon Him whose own Father poured out curses so we could receive blessings.

PAUSE AND REFLECT

1. This is too great to skim over, too powerful to reduce to hindsight. In light of Deuteronomy 21:23, do you believe that God's curse fell on Jesus as He hung on the cross?

2. Admit to Jesus if/how the act of Him willingly being cursed by His Father affects you. It's okay. He can fully handle it.

3. We will never appreciate the enormity of the cross if we attempt to minimize it. Sit. Wrestle. Scream. Do what it takes, but make the time today to let your mind—and your heart—experience the deep agony, pain, and sorrow.

Might I also suggest a prayer of gratitude that stems from the deepest parts within? I'll offer a springboard if you need it:

Oh, Jesus, I will never, ever, understand what you did for me. It makes me squirm because I want to believe that I'm a pretty good person and that you made my whiteness a little whiter while really helping those other people. Oh, but Jesus, I am they, aren't I? You know how my thoughts don't bring you the glory you deserve, how I fixate on the wrong things, making more money, how to get ahead, or so many other things. Jesus, if I'm honest, I'm a pretty big mess. I really can't understand why you would love me so much that you would let your Father curse you because of me and for my benefit. I'm not sure I'll ever fully understand it, but even if I don't, please don't ever let me forget it.

Jesus, these words are feeble in light of everything you've done for me, but thank you. From the deepest parts within me, thank you. You are my King. The lover of my soul, and the One who guides my path. Oh, how I love you.

Amen.

DAY 30. RECEIVING MORE THAN JESUS

"Never will I leave you. Never will I forsake you." Hebrews 13:5 offers this rich promise filled with hope and confidence.

Never, as in not for one little second, will we be left alone. Ever. We could stop right there and call it good, reveling in the incomprehensible knowledge that the Almighty promises to never leave us nor forsake us.

We could, but we shouldn't, for if we dig a little deeper, this incredible promise becomes even more pronounced. Are you ready for it? I scarce can take it in, and honestly I'm stalling before committing these words to paper. They hurt too much to admit, but I'll just blurt it out.

We bask in the promise that He "will neither leave nor forsake us" while Jesus could not. Yes, you read that right. We are afforded something the Son of Man, God's own son, was not,

Think about some of Jesus' final words on the cross. As He struggled for those final breaths. Jesus would have had to use the last of his strength to call out:

"My God, my God, why have you forsaken me?"

No, this wasn't an emotional outburst expressing how Jesus *felt*. This was the truth of what was actually transpiring the moment when God, His Father, turned away from Him and He experienced the absence of God.

Yesterday we learned about the shame of the cross and how it brought the curse of God. As if that wasn't bad enough, it gets worse. Much, much worse.

Jesus' point in allowing Himself to be sacrificed on the cross was to serve as the pure sacrificial lamb that took upon Himself all the sins of the world.

All! My mind can't even begin to comprehend something of that magnitude.

My sin is bad enough, but then toss in yours *and all* sins of *all* people who lived, now live, and will live until the day He returns. Tack on all the selfishness, lewdness, and *every* wrong against God and his fellow man and then suddenly this forsaking thing starts making sense. Jesus became so filthy with our stuff—my stuff!!—that God could no longer look at Him and had to momentarily turn His back.

This is the very place where the deepest sense of love abounds. Do you see it? Jesus' compassion was so deep that He allowed our grime to cover every aspect of His being, and to such an extent that the One He'd walked with since the beginning of time turned His back and ear to Him. He watched in horror as His son was tortured and unmercifully slain so that we may mercifully live.

All this so His incredible promise that He could not offer to Jesus could be extended to you and me.

"Never will I leave you. Never will I forsake you."

PAUSE AND REFLECT

1. Has there ever been a time when you really needed someone's support in either a literal sense or figurative sense? If you did receive it, what would have happened if you didn't? If you didn't receive it, what happened? How would the outcome have been different if you weren't alone?

2. What does it mean to you know that God has promised to never leave you nor forsake you?

3. Does Hebrews 13:5 take on a new meaning in light of Jesus' words of "My God, my God, why have you forsaken me?" If so, how do you now view it?

DAY 31. JAB, PUNCH, CRY

Laughter filled the room as Gabe and I wrestled one evening. Our friends' kids were staying with us for the week, so the semi-inflated air mattress lying on the floor just begged for a fun mother-son feud. When I tickled him, the mattress propelled Gabe upwards, his arms flailing every which way, including the direction of my face.

I fell backwards, clutching my jaw and knowing I'd lost the title in this mom versus son battle. Tears streamed down my face despite my attempts to will them away. Kids—both mine and my friends'—stared at me in confusion and fear, knowing I'm not one to burst into tears in front of them. But burst I did.

All of them asked if they could do something for me, but the pain was so severe that I just needed some time to lay down and hope it would soon go away.

"I'm. Going. To. Room," I grunted as each syllable added to the pain.

I popped some Ibuprofen and laid down, but the sounds of five restless, unattended kids lured me downstairs. I kept my words to a minimum as I heard popping noises every time I moved my mouth, followed by more tears.

Finally, I admitted defeat. "Sorry. Everyone bed. Now. I sleep. Too much pain. G'night."

With that attempt at removing myself for the evening, I shut my bedroom door and let the tears flow.

At least for a few seconds.

"Um, Miss Stacy, sorry to disturb you. I know this might sound selfish, but it really isn't fair that the boys get the bigger air mattress. I mean, we're older than them, so we should have it. Could you tell them to trade with us and then carry theirs down to the family room for us and take the smaller one up to them?"

I've known this girl for years and have a great relationship with her, but the pain I felt at that moment—a pain compounded whenever I spoke or climbed stairs—trumped the desire for tact or compassion.

"No. Can't," I said, shutting my bedroom door. I didn't want to be rude and under other circumstances I would have considered her request or at least explained my reason for rejecting it, but the pain from talking was too much to bear.

If my jaw hurt that bad just from bumping into an eight-year-old on a mattress, then think about how Jesus must have felt after each of the following:

> "Then they spit in his face and struck him with their fists. Others slapped him." Matthew 26:67

> "Then some began to spit at him; they blindfolded him, struck him with their fists, and said, 'Prophesy!' And the guards took him and beat him." Mark 14:65

> "They spit on him, and took the staff and struck him on the head again and again." Matthew 27:30

Can you imagine being slapped, spit on, hit while blindfolded, and being struck with a staff over and over? My brain can't comprehend that level of pain, which doesn't even account for the anguish of having a crown of thorns pressed against His brow and nails driven through His wrists and ankles.

If that was me, I'd be doing good to mutter a few words here and there, yet Jesus said, "Father, forgive them, for they know not what they do" (Luke 23:34).

It's unthinkable, like dreaming about a new car for years, only to hand the keys over to a stranger within seconds of receiving it. But that's just the beginning.

Luke 23:34 is written in the imperfect tense, the verb form used when something occurs over and over.

Father, forgive them.

Father, forgive them.

Father, forgive them.

The physical anguish was vast, yet perhaps there was something even more compelling that pushed Jesus past the pain in order to recite these heart-breaths over and over:

We need to know we're forgiven.

We need to know we're forgiven.

We need to know we're forgiven.

Jesus begged for our pardon at a time and place that seems unlikely. The timing seems off because He asked for the forgiveness of the people who put Him to death—*as they were putting Him to death.* We're told that time can heal, yet it was only through the *untimely* act of forgiveness—offering it in the moment since He had few left—that others were healed.

The place was unheard of, too. I'm more of a forgive-someone-from-the-comforts-of-my-bed type, a chew on it for a while and then quietly release the hurt without the offending party being aware of it. Yet Jesus freely offered His forgiveness, even when He could barely breathe. Don't forget that death by crucifixion meant asphyxiation. Someone dying that way had to push up into the cross to draw another breath, so the effort to do so *and* say something would have been exponentially harder.

But He did it, pain and all.

Why?

Because as He faced death, He chose to offer life.

PAUSE AND REFLECT

1. Think about a time your mouth hurt. Perhaps it was from a trip to the dentist's office, or maybe from bumping into something or taking a blow to the face. How did you respond? Did you want to talk anytime soon after it happened?

2. "Sorry, but I have to save my words for my family," a friend said after recovering from multiple surgeries to battle the cancer in her mouth. It hurt so much to talk that she only said what was most important—and to whom it was most important. How does that apply with Jesus' final words: "Father, forgive them"?

We don't need to save our words. Even if it's hard to articulate, don't forget to let your spirit utter a response to the words cried out on our behalf.

Jesus, I don't understand the pain you endured, the shame you faced, or the heartache of it all. I also don't understand that you say I'm worthy of forgiveness. Help me to accept it. Help me to accept it. Help me to accept it. Amen.

3. How does the fact that Jesus offered forgiveness to the very people who were responsible for putting Him

to death challenge you with regards to forgiving others? What impact does it make on any belief you might have held about the *time* and *place* in which we should offer forgiveness?

4. Is it your time and place to offer forgiveness to someone who desperately needs it? Perhaps you need to release them, even if for your own benefit. Maybe you need to forgive yourself. Whatever the case, if you're being prompted to release your hurts or disappointments, don't dismiss it.

DAY 32. DARKNESS

I'm not a cave-exploring junkie, but I've lived in enough places near underground worlds filled with stalactites and stalagmites that I've spent more time in these subterranean places than most. I've trekked through caves throughout Mexico, as well as some in Utah, Colorado, New Mexico, and South Dakota. The differences between them are amazing. A few have delicate art forms on the walls, a result of running water mixing with limestone. Some are moist and damp, while others are dry and cool. Some have stalactites stretching downward and others have smooth floors and ceilings.

The tours of these caves varied as much as the caves themselves. Some were in English. Others in Spanish. Some guides pointed out geological formations, while others commented on their interpretation of who they thought certain shapes looked like, much like playing the game of looking at the clouds and trying to spot a dog or a rabbit. Despite these differences, there is one part that is the same in every tour.

"Get ready," the guide states. "I'm going to turn off the lights and let you see how dark it is down here. You might want to hold onto the handrails to steady yourself."

Yeah, like a little darkness is going to make me fall, I inwardly chuckled the first time I heard the suggestion. Besides, the cave was, well, a cave. It was already dark.

Or so I thought.

> We walk in darkness yet never feel the full effects of it because light came in and guided the way.

When the lights went out, sheer and utter darkness enveloped me, a kind of blackness I rarely experience. The first time I was in a subterranean cavern and the guide flipped off the lights, I became dizzy and swayed back and forth in the darkness. I held my arm out to balance myself—and couldn't even see it.

Caves are naturally dark, but the family tours I've taken are rigged with artificial lighting. Mind you, it isn't exactly bright, but it definitely isn't dark. It sounds like our world, doesn't it? We can't even make it to the fourth chapter in the Bible without hearing of people lying to God and killing their own relatives.

We walk in that darkness, yet never feel the full effects of it because, like the cave, light came in and guided the way. Jesus said, “I am the light of the world” (John 8:12), but Someone flipped off the switch during Jesus’ final three hours on the cross, and “darkness came over all the land” (Matthew 27:45).

The light prepared to leave this world and descend into the deepest darkness so that we may have the light of life.

PAUSE AND REFLECT

1. I’m a lover of light, setting up my desk as close to natural sunlight as possible. I tend to gloss over the darkness in the Easter story because I know what’s about to come, the thing I gravitate to like a moth: light. But today, right now, let’s attempt to shield our minds from the knowledge that hindsight gives but wasn’t available to those at the foot of the cross. Block out the light as much as possible, if even for a brief moment. Light a candle in a bathroom or place without windows and then blow it out. Find the pitchest of black and let its effects dizzy you, and set you back in confusion.

2. If you manage to find some semblance of darkness, awaken your senses to the effect it has, or imagine you are alone in the mountains as night falls. Are you more fearful? Do you have a clear sense of direction?

Without using any type of flashlight, candle, GPS, or device, how will you find your way out?

3. It is hard to find absolute darkness in our society. In fact, I write this from my backyard and am constantly moving my chair in an attempt to stay in the shade. We have flashlight apps on our phones, lanterns when we camp, headlights on our cars, and streetlights lining the sidewalks. Darkness is nearly foreign, but the best appreciation for what we have comes from recognizing what it would be like without it. Say a prayer thanking God for the light He brings you. I'll get you started if you need a jumping board:

Jesus, thank you for not only being the light of the world, but for being my light, the One who promises to direct my steps. Help me remember how dark and bleak my world was before I met you. Help me realize what my life would be like if it weren't for you, and then use that knowledge to embrace your light more fully. Amen.

DAY 33. THE UNTORN CLOAK

A Narrative

I thought it was my lucky day. I've never won anything before, so when we started casting lots, I played along with everyone else while knowing the result would be the same as always: nothing.

But boy, was I wrong that day.

Or maybe very right. I'm not sure which.

I won alright. Did I ever! I didn't win just any old coat, mind you. Nuh, uh. It was one of those fancy kinds. You know, the garments that are a single piece without any seams.

That's why we cast lots for it, the whole no-seam thing. If we tried tearing it, we'd rip it to bits so we played a little game to see who would get that fancy jacket.

You can only imagine my surprise when the lot fell on me. Me, the person who has never won a thing in his life!

Now that jacket taunts me, it's lack of seams drawing even more attention to the many things that have torn lately. You heard about those ripped things, didn't you?

I heard the curtain of the temple, the one that blocks anyone from entering the Holy of Holies, was completely torn in two, top to bottom. Someone said it ripped at the exact moment that man breathed His last and died. It's as if God Himself reached down and tore it. That curtain was sixty feet high and four inches thick. How can they possibly repair that? Now that it's torn in two, I wonder what they will do since the barricade no longer exists.

The irony is too great to ignore. We didn't want to tear that man's garment for it was of great worth, yet I was fine with His body being torn as the flogging ripped chunks of skin off His back.

Of course, the irony goes even deeper. That garment was like those of a high priest, who were the only people allowed into the Holy of Holies, and even they could only enter under special circumstances. Yet now with the veil torn, anyone can walk right into the sacred.

The rocks split that day, too. Creepiest thing I ever did see. Large boulders broke into two while dead people came out of the earth and started walking around.

My heart broke when I saw all of this.

What have I done? Did I really approve of an innocent man's death?

There is no fixing this heart, riddled as it is with guilt and anguish. I fear it will remain torn, just like that curtain . . .

Author's Note: I am purposely cutting this one short, allowing it to end at a place that is uncomfortable. It doesn't resemble a proper ending simply because that is part of the great mystery of the cross, the struggle between what is in that moment and what is to come; what is seen versus what happens later.

PAUSE AND REFLECT

1. Do you ever feel like your heart is too riddled with guilt to be able to enter into the throne room of Christ?

2. What does it mean to you that the veil was torn—top to bottom!—removing the barrier that stood between God and man?

3. Imagine being in the temple not long after the veil was torn. Would you feel worthy to enter into the Holy of Holies? If you answered no as I did, then let's

challenge ourselves to embrace the gift of the cross—the ability to enter—even when (or especially when) our hearts are torn by the realization of and repentance for our inadequacies and sinfulness.

4. Where is the story of your life in comparison to the Easter story? Do you feel like:

- You're standing beside the cross, a world of disappointment, hurt and frustration in front of you,
- Easter morning, filled with the similar confusion and uncertainty that the Marys experienced as they searched for Jesus' body,
- Shouts of "He's Alive!" permeate your surroundings as you rejoice in the unimaginable coming to life,
- Somewhere in between, or
- A combination of the above

DAY 34. IT IS FINISHED

"He said he was going to fly on a plane," Gabe announced.

"He who?" I asked, confused as I usually am when my little guy starts a new conversation without letting me know who or what he is referring to. It happens so frequently that I stumbled upon a code phrase that lets Gabe know I don't have a clue what he's talking about.

"How was it?"

"Huh?" Gabe asks, his mouth gaping in confusion.

"How was it?" I'll ask again. Then the look of understanding crosses his face as he realizes I didn't explain the subject of my conversation, just like he failed to do.

"Oh, so what I meant to say is that Tommy said he was going to fly . . ." Gabe explains.

I'm a word girl, so I want my kids to give me the tools I need to track with what they're saying. I usually need the same thing when conversing with others, but there is one instance when someone started a new conversation with a pronoun and it made absolute sense. Jesus' final words before breathing His last:

"It is finished" (John 19:30).

What was the "it"?

Did it mean the torture of the cross?

Maybe it referred to the separation, the division between God and man that was never intended to be there. Or maybe He was referring to the division between the life Jesus came to give us and the one we actually live out. Perhaps it was about the longing, the hoping, the *less-than-ness* of life.

Was He referring to His anguish?

Maybe He meant ours.

Whatever it was, or is, the beautiful truth is that in Christ all of these things and so much more are finished.

PAUSE AND REFLECT

1. Have you ever worked on a project for so long that by the time it was completed you celebrated the fact that it was done? How did you feel once you could say, "It is finished"?

2. What do you think Jesus was referring to when He said, "It is finished"?

3. Those who complete a marathon without placing in the top of their age group receive a medal that says "Finisher." I used to think that was a pathetic reward for such a grueling task, but once I completed a similar feat myself, I understood the pride in just being able to state that I saw it through. Think about the words "It is finished" from Jesus' vantage point. Perhaps He meant the years of forfeiting the beauty of heaven to walk on earth, the many times the Pharisees tried to catch Him or trip Him up, the betrayal He experienced, and the separation He experienced from His Father had ended, both for Himself and for us.

DAY 35. LAST WILL AND TESTAMENT

A young girl lost her dad much too young.

“Did he leave me anything in his will?” she asked. She’d seen several movies in which someone’s will was read and she perceived it as a silent proclamation of who mattered in the deceased person’s life and who didn’t make the cut. She was too young to know the in’s and outs of final testaments, but her little heart desperately needed to know if her father took the time to pen her name into his final words.

The short answer: yes.

The long answer: he left an estate in the red and a lapsed life insurance policy.

“It might take some time,” the girl’s mom told her, “but you’ll definitely get some of dad’s things.” The girl’s arm instantly shot into the air as a signal to stop, silencing her mom.

“I just wanted to know he thought of me and included me.” Her little face that had been wrinkled with crevices of grief and anguish since the death of her father now relaxed in peace.

He had remembered. Of course he remembered. He was her daddy, and she was his little girl.

She missed her daddy and no piece of paper could change that, but in that instant, the question that every girl (and most of us women) asks over and over received its best answer: she mattered.

Wills aren't written haphazardly. Countless scenarios are considered and include remedies for nearly every possible hypothetical situation. Jesus' last will was no different. He thought through every provision, every exception, every *person.* Then he wrote a will that accounted for all of those "what-ifs," and sealed it through the covenant of His blood.

Don't let the cross be far removed. Let its truth ring triumphantly. You mattered. I mattered. We did then, and we still do today.

PAUSE AND REFLECT

1. Have you ever wondered if someone remembered you, or bumped into a friend and it was obvious they couldn't recall your name?

2. Can you relate to wondering if you matter? If so, how?

3. How can Jesus' work on the cross prove without a doubt that you are important to God? Are there portions of Scripture that prove to you the intentionality of the cross (hint: if you can't think of any, skim over the last few days for some clues!).

DAY 36. DO YOU UNDERSTAND?

A Narrative from the disciple John

Ah, I remember the day like it was yesterday. Beautiful blue sky, pleasant cooling breeze, and lots of fish. In fact, there were so many fish that my brother James and I had to mend our nets after the catch. As we repaired those old nets yet again, He called out to my brother and me. You know. Him. Jesus. "Hey John, James. Come here."

I didn't really understand, but I followed Him anyway. There was just something about Him. Nothing physical of course. He looked just like everyone else, but there was something in His eyes. I can't really describe it, but it was like He knew. . . knew me. Knew God. Was God. So James and I followed Him.

Not too long ago, tears streamed down Mary Magdalene's face as she kissed and washed Jesus' feet. She poured the most amazing smelling perfume on His feet. It must have cost a year's wages, but lavish it on she did.

I really didn't understand why Mary did that. After all, there were people there whose job was to wash the feet of guests. Even if she felt like she needed to assume that role, did she really need such expensive perfume? I kept waiting for Jesus to chastise her, but He didn't. In fact, He told her that her many sins had been forgiven.

Tonight Jesus did the same thing for me. He didn't use expensive perfume, but the realization that the Son of God washed the grime off my feet was enough to do me in. As He cupped my soiled foot, a flood of tears threatened to completely destroy my illusion of composure.

Later that night, Jesus went to one of His favorite spots at the Mount of Olives, and as usual we followed. We tried to stay awake as he asked us to, but we were all so tired that we quickly fell asleep. I didn't realize that Jesus was so overwhelmed with anguish that His sweat was like drops of blood.

When He returned, He found us asleep. He woke us just as a crowd approached Judas leading them. I couldn't believe it. They had come to take my Jesus away! Why did He let them? Sure, there were a lot more of them, but we could have at least tried. Peter tried and drew his sword, but Jesus told him to put it away. Why? There had been times when people tried to stone Jesus and He escaped by simply slipping through the crowd. Why didn't He even try to do that? I don't understand.

I was there when Pilate brought Jesus out before the crowd. It was madness. Some of the very same people that Jesus had cured of leprosy or had cast demons out of were part of the forming mob, forgetting what Jesus had done for them. Caught up in the craziness of it all, everyone stopped thinking rationally and got swept away. "Crucify Him," they screamed. "Crucify Him."

Crucify? My Jesus? They wanted to crucify Him? Why?

I wish I could have done something. I tried to think of a plan, some way to free Jesus, but in the end I knew nothing would work. Jesus didn't fight or struggle, almost as if he didn't want to be freed. He just took it.

What happened next is too horrific to fully describe. I'm sure you'll hear about all that they did to Him in the days to come. There was blood. A lot of it. It ran down His face when they mocked Him by driving a crown of thorns on His head. They beat him, whipped him so violently that pieces of flesh fell off His back.

Why didn't He stop it? I know He was the Son of God and had the power to do something to save himself from this, but instead He just took it. Why would He do that?

My heart was sick as I watched Him struggle to carry His cross. I wished I could have taken His place, for I have no purpose here anymore without Him.

Jesus was so weak from the flogging that He could no longer carry the cross, so they grabbed someone from the crowd and made him carry it for Him. Jesus just kept walking, straight towards the place where they would strip Him of what little life remained in Him.

Part of me kept hoping Jesus was waiting until the last minute and would then do something spectacular to save Himself. He never did. He just hung there, nailed to a cross, struggling just to breathe as he waited to die. He took it all.

Even through all the suffering and pain, He never said anything against them. Just took it. It was like . . . like . . . part. . . of. . . His. . . plan. Part of His plan!

Oh, I understand it now. He didn't take it. No one made Him do any it. He didn't take it, He gave it! Do you understand? It was His plan all along. He gave His life for us. For me. For you. Do you understand?

PAUSE AND REFLECT

1. Is there anything about Jesus' life or crucifixion that you don't understand? Maybe something your mind can grasp, but your heart can't comprehend?

2. There are countless instances throughout the gospels where the disciples didn't understand what Jesus said. How does it impact you knowing that the people closest

to Jesus didn't understand what He said or why? How does that encourage you regarding the areas of faith you can't understand?

3. This narrative ends with one of the most important questions we must answer: do we understand? The cross wasn't an accident, and its gift wasn't given for a select few. Some of us understand that, while others do not. Take time today to make sure you know your answer to this fundamental question.

DAY 37. WHEN THE LIGHT BURST

What happens when the only thing illuminating the darkness is extinguished? It gets dark, of course. Watch as science and faith intersect:

> "From noon until three in the afternoon darkness came over all the land." Matthew 27:45

Could it be that as Christ hung on the cross, the light of the World's flame flickered? If this happened late at night, it wouldn't have been notable, but it occurred during the hottest part of the day. The earth dressed itself in mourning at the loss of its Creator.

This will come as no surprise to you, but I love a good story. I don't just visualize or hear about events taking place, but quickly connect each detail with emotions I feel must have been triggered by what was happening. Indulge me as I go to where my heart leads when I think about when the earth was enveloped in darkness in the middle of the day for three hours.

Strange, right? Absolutely! But what about the return of the "un-dark?" Was it a slow warming of the sun? Did beautiful rays of light illuminate the sky with shades of orange, pink, and purple? That doesn't make much sense to me. Sunrise at 3 p.m.?

Some try to explain what happened by saying it was a solar eclipse. That could have been the case, except there wasn't darkness during the eclipse I witnessed. I have my own theory. It will never be confirmed by scientists or theologians, but it stretches my thinking just the same. Take a virtual tour of the temple with me as I present my hypothesis.

Inside the temple were literal barriers. One barrier was a short wall designating the place where Gentiles were not allowed to pass. Another was the well-known divider which separated the Holy of Holies from everything else. The High Priest was the only one allowed beyond this barrier and only on one day of the year on the Day of Atonement. When he entered, he did so with a rope tied around his ankle in case the presence of the Lord struck him dead (yes, truly, so they could drag the dead priest out by his ankle to bury him—let that one settle in for a minute!).

I don't think the barrier was something most people wanted removed. I mean, if a High Priest could die in the Holy of Holies, what chance did an average person have of surviving that kind of direct contact with God?

What I visualize is like the time I took my kids to Black Canyon of the Gunnison National Park. It's a magnificent sight to behold, yet touring it stressed me to no end when I saw my little guy running to and fro on loose sand near the edge of a deep cavern. I grabbed his hand and wouldn't let go until I had him safely back inside the minivan. Okay, so maybe he was actually feet from the edge but in this mom's eye, that was still too close. Why? Because death is real.

It was that same perception of danger and fear of death that kept people comfortable on the outside of that barrier. The significance of the Holy of Holies can fill many books (and, in fact, it has), but suffice it to say that the barrier didn't exist because God is mean. It was there because sin cannot live in the presence of God and man (before Jesus) was unclean with sin.

That's the beauty of Easter. Our Savior was anything but clean in that moment of death. Whips tore the flesh from Christ's body. Blood streamed down from the crown of thorns that pierced his brow and the stakes hammered into his hands and feet to attach Him to the cross. But that's just the surface filth. The real uncleanliness came at the moment all our sins fell on Him, taking all of our junk to the grave. That's the backdrop. Listen in to what happened during those hours of darkness:

"From noon until three in the afternoon darkness came over all the land. About three in the afternoon Jesus cried out in a loud voice, 'Eli, Eli, lema sabachthani?' (which means "My God, my God, why have you forsaken me?")

When some of those standing there heard this, they said, 'He's calling Elijah.'

Immediately one of them ran and got a sponge. He filled it with wine vinegar, put it on a staff, and offered it to Jesus to drink. The rest said, 'Now leave him alone. Let's see if Elijah comes to save him.'

And when Jesus had cried out again in a loud voice, he gave up his spirit.

At that moment the curtain of the temple was torn in two from top to bottom. The earth shook, the rocks split and the tombs broke open. The bodies of many holy people who had died were raised to life. They came out of the tombs after Jesus' resurrection and went into the holy city and appeared to many people." Matthew 27:45-53

Here's how my brain sees the parts Matthew didn't record: Jesus died, paying the ultimate price, and in that same instant, **we became clean**. Read: holy (mind blowing, right?).

In that moment, there was no longer a need to separate holy from holy, so the curtain creating the barrier was torn in two, from top to bottom. It was like heaven reached down and flicked that thick fabric away, just as easily as I squash a fruit fly.

In that same second when the *once-holy-turned-filthy-because-of-us* died, that filth was removed from us. He purchased (redeemed) us in the most costly way possible, making us clean in the presence of God. So the temple veil was torn, the barrier removed, and light flooded the Holy of Holies.

The light burst forth from the temple for there was no longer a barrier confining it. Darkness ceased as light poured into the blackest crevices of the earth, even spilling into the tombs where once-dead people had slept.

I have ventured deep into the realm of conjecture, trying to show you what stirs my heart. But this much we can know beyond a shadow of a doubt: the Light of the World shone bright—and still does.

PAUSE AND REFLECT

1. Think about a time when you were in complete blackness. How did you feel? Were you disoriented? Scared?

2. What do you think about my theory? It's ok to think its bunk. If you disagree, how do you imagine the darkness broke?

3. Regardless of any theories of how light came back into the world after Jesus died, the undisputable fact is that the veil separating that which was holy tore and allowed that which wasn't holy to enter. That sure seems like something we need to shine the light on as we pause and thank God for that incredible gift—the gift of bringing us into His presence.

DAY 38. MOURNING THE LOSS

My church held a Good Friday service where we walked through the stations of the cross (commemoration of fourteen events as Jesus carried his cross to Calvary). It was a powerful experience that incorporated sound, sight, and touch to remember Christ's journey towards His ultimate sacrifice. The evening was powerful, yet I never could have prepared myself for the way it ended.

The last station was in the worship center where we were given the chance to reflect upon all that Christ endured on our behalf. Although I sit there most Sundays, this particular night was different, carrying me back to six weeks earlier when I sat in that same place for my former boss's memorial.

Cancer cut Doug's days short, causing him to pass when he was only fifty years old. Despite the brevity of his life, each of those years were lived with meaning and intentionality.

That kind of living innately draws others in, which was evidenced throughout Doug's memorial service. In fact, that's the reason it was held in the large sanctuary of the church I attend because the smaller church that Doug and his family called home could not accommodate all the people whose lives he touched.

The room was packed, every seat occupied. An entire school cancelled classes since almost everyone would be at the service.

It was a celebration of life, a recounting of the legacy Doug created during his too-short life. But let's be clear. While there was laughter splattered here and there as people remembered Doug and relied on each other to embrace the overwhelming challenge of this thing called life, grief predominated.

How could it not?

Death comes with a horrible sting for those left behind, especially when it's the passing of a vibrant life that was embraced and poured out on others.

As I sat in the worship center that Good Friday, I felt the weight of death in a way I had never experienced before. When I finally lifted my head to watch the person on the stage tenderly worshipping in remembrance, I saw it:

A body. Wrapped in linens. Lying across a table.

Lifeless.

Yes, what I looked at wasn't a real body, but when I saw it in the exact spot where we mourned a dynamic individual only weeks before, something profound struck me in that moment.

What we deem as good, is. This Friday *is* good, but only in light of the years lived prior to it *and* the days that came after. But this day, viewed just in itself, feels anything but good. Instead, it is heavy. Dark. And riddled with feelings of grief and loss.

I want so much to tell you more about Doug's funeral and his life, sharing some of those beautiful nuggets that challenged and inspired so many. I want so much to fast forward a few days when I will sit in this auditorium again and hear the pastor declare, "He is risen," to which we all reply, "He is risen indeed."

The morning of Doug's funeral I woke up with a feeling of dread, wanting to find some excuse to miss the service and put off the acceptance of a loss I wish never happened. That same feeling arises when I realize I cannot simply skip the part about Christ's pain, suffering, and death and instead race to the celebration. But just like I willed myself to put on a black dress and attend the sad event I wished to avoid, I will drape myself in the veil of mourning this Good Friday and allow myself to sit uncomfortably in the shadows of death.

Let me remember the unforeseen blessings I would have missed if I had avoided the funeral of my friend that day. And as I allow myself to experience the pain and grief of Christ's death, let me remember the unforeseen blessings of what transpired that day on the cross, and the seen blessings of what is to come.

Come join me.

PAUSE AND REFLECT

1. Think about a loss you've experienced. For some it could be a parent or close relative. Perhaps a few are fortunate enough to have never lost anyone close yet. If so, think about a time when you had to put a pet down or lost something dear. How did you feel? No, how did you *really* feel? Was it hard to breathe? Was it nearly impossible to get out of bed? Did you cry all day or hold back the tears, fearful that if they started, they might never stop?

2. Have you ever been in a situation that was eerie or something happened contrary to the norm? How did that make you feel? Did your pulse race and your palms get sweaty? Think about how you would have felt as each of the following happened during Christ's crucifixion:

> "Now from noon until three, darkness came all over the land" (Matthew 27:45).

> "Just then the temple curtain was torn in two, from top to bottom. The earth shook and the rocks were split apart. And tombs were opened, and the bodies of many saints who had died were raised" (Matthew 27:52).

3. Today unfortunately is the day when we need to stop and let Christ's death sink in. He wasn't in a long sleep, waiting to be awakened again on Sunday. Jesus died.

I challenge you to let yourself feel the weight of that truth today. Let the grief overwhelm and the gratitude pour out.

DAY 39. THE THIRD QUARTER

For those of you who are like me and are not huge sports fans, let me give you a quick overview of Super Bowl 51. The New England Patriots were favored to win over the Atlanta Falcons, yet they never managed to have more points on the scoreboard than their opponents throughout most of the game. In fact, midway through the third quarter, they were a full 25 points behind the Falcons.

Many rejoiced as they cheered on the underdog. Others sulked. Some even left the stadium, relinquishing the seats they paid a lot of money for.

That's how the Saturday wedged between Good Friday and Resurrection Sunday feels, or at least how I imagine it felt at that time for those who didn't have the benefit of hindsight like we do.

For some, their hopes were dashed. Despair ran deep. Sorrow and confusion saturated every thought.

What just happened?

How did this happen?

In short, a crushing defeat.

But let's be real. Not everyone grieved Jesus' death. It would be illogical to think that those chanting "Crucify! Crucify!" suddenly mourned the very outcome they petitioned for.

> From a third quarter perspective, it looked like Jesus had lost the game.

The Pharisees and other religious leaders celebrated that the threat to their set-in-stone ways was gone.

And let's not forget that other dimension we can't see, but dare not overlook: the spiritual plane between good and evil. Just like the Falcons' fans who whooped, hollered, and cheered their almost certain victory, so did Satan and his forces.

Ok, so it's not just like that. The Falcons were about to win a victory that would crown them football champions for only a year until other teams vied for the title. The winner of the life-and-death battle between Friday and Sunday would determine the fate of billions of people from that moment forward, an outcome that would last well beyond a mere 365 days.

Jesus made it clear He had to die and would rise again on the third day. His disciples and other followers didn't comprehend that. Did Satan and his followers?

I'm not about to take a stab at the thoughts of the devil, but I have no doubt that Satan is thoroughly acquainted with the Scriptures and Christ's words. How else would he have been able to quote scripture to Jesus when he tempted Him in the desert? The New Testament hadn't yet been penned, but Matthew 16:21 says, "from that time on Jesus began to explain to his disciples that he must go to Jerusalem and suffer many things at the hands of the elders, chief priests and teachers of the law, and that he must be killed and on the third day be raised to life." Would Satan have been aware of this?

If so, my guess is that Saturday was a day he tried to keep Jesus in the tomb and made every effort to undo what had been prophesied. It was a day to make Jesus' predictions as inaccurate as the forecasts that the Patriots would win—or at least faulty when viewed from a third quarter perspective.

Because from the third quarter view, it looked like both had lost the game.

But it's not over until it's over . . . or until the massive stone gets rolled away.

PAUSE AND REFLECT

1. If you watched the 2017 Super Bowl, how did you feel during the third quarter? If you didn't watch it, have you ever been in a game or experienced something that seemed doomed to fail? Think about how you felt during that time.

2. Let yourself feel the weight of defeat—the defeat Christ's followers undoubtedly felt, that is. Don't skip to the celebration of tomorrow yet.

3. Have you lived a season in the third quarter, a time when it looks as if all is lost? If you're there now, first let me say I'm sorry. I've been there too, and I know it's crazy hard. But let me also encourage you to look beyond the scoreboard of your life, for we know something that those who watched Jesus breathe His last didn't understand: we serve a God who knows that deep-down, soul-crushing sorrow. That same God knows how to take something that looks like utter defeat and flip it on its head in the most extraordinary way.

4. At the end of a 91-yard drive, the Patriots scored a touchdown and a two-point conversion, tying the game with less a minute left on the clock. They made history as the Super Bowl went into overtime for the first time.

If you were watching a game similar to Super Bowl 51 in which it appeared that one team had locked up the game, but then the other team began making a huge comeback, what would you do? More specifically, what would you do if others didn't know about the comeback? Would you share the news with them so they, too, could see the outcome?

It isn't too late to invite someone to the celebration of the greatest win ever. A poll from Lifeway Research shows that seven out of ten people said they would attend church if someone invited them.

DAY 40. CELEBRATING THE LIVING

Some would call it writer's block, but I know better. I sit here at a complete loss trying to find some analogy to Christ's resurrection. I thought about the aquarium fish we thought got sucked into the filter after it died, only to see him swim out once we turned off the filter. I considered telling the story about my friend's husband who walked out of the hospital and went home after a flesh-eating staph infection nearly took his life.

But here's the thing. There is nothing that could possibly compare with the ultimate sacrifice, not a little fish that almost died, or even my friend's recovery, as miraculous as it was.

This is no block. It's simply that there is nothing to liken it to because there has never been nor will there ever be anything remotely close to the resurrection. After all, Jesus was dead.

Let me repeat.

Dead, as in wrapped in 75-100 pounds of spices laid between the cloths covering Him from head to foot. Dead, as in placed in a tomb.

And yet not so very dead. Not today, Resurrection Sunday or on any other day from that day forward. Today is the day we shed the coverings of death and the grief that accompanies it. Today we switch from mourning death to celebrating life.

But it's more than that, more than Jesus coming back to life (which is the greatest event in the world's history). This is about something even bigger, something so immense that I don't have a clue how to take it in. But whether I comprehend it or not, the truth is we celebrate one who lived, died, and then lived again so that we can also live, die, and then live again.

But here's the sad truth: some of us won't. None of us will cheat death, but it's the life on either side of death that comes into question. You see, for as much as I celebrate Easter, swinging my kids around in sheer joy and saying, "He's alive!" over and over again, today also holds a sadness and a penetrating challenge.

The One whose resurrected life we celebrate spoke to us about life, both on this side and the other. "I have come that they may have life," He said, "and have it to the full." John 10:10

To live a monotone, "Eeyore-ish" life in the doldrums reduces this gift to something so much less than it was ever intended to be.

But let's be real: a reduced gift is better than no gift at all. I don't say that to justify a life of safety or complaining. The worst way to diminish this present is to never accept it. If you haven't yet, it's easier than you can imagine (the accepting part, that is). I'm not about to tell you that living it out is a cakewalk, though, or that you'll be immune from hardships. Accepting it simply means you recognize you've done things that are less than or contrary to what God wants. This isn't just about the big things like murder or adultery. It's also about being selfish and putting your own needs before anyone else's or spouting off on your kids when you were too tired, or a million other different things.

We've all been there. *Are* there. That's the beauty of the gift we were given: we can own what we've done, but rather than using it as a way to declare we aren't worthy, those things become the very reason we need it and are eligible to receive it.

Romans 10:9-10 tells us the rest:

> "If you declare with your mouth, 'Jesus is Lord,' and believe in your heart that God raised him from the dead, you will be saved. For it is with your heart that you believe and are justified, and it is with your mouth that you profess your faith and are saved."

Who knows, today just might be the day we celebrate more than one restored life!

PAUSE AND REFLECT

1. It's time for a pulse check: how's your living going? Is it monotonous and boring, full and abundant, or somewhere in between? If you aren't happy with your answer, what is one baby step you can implement today to change that?

2. How's your post-death life looking? Are you certain of where you'll spend the endless years and millennia after you die? If you don't like your answer, I've already given you the outline for how to know beyond a shadow of a doubt where you'll be. Oh how I hope you accept it if you haven't yet!

3. I'd be amiss if we didn't stop to truly savor this ultimate gift. Let it sink deep. Relive the pain and then celebrate the unthinkable: a huge, massive stone rolled away to reveal something even more incredible: a power to defeat something as permanent as death.

SECTION II

LIVING THE RESURRECTION

DAY 41. EASTER RACES

I love running. Give me a pair of shoes and some music and I'm good for an hour or more. I've been running for decades, which might be why I love the Easter races from that first resurrection Sunday.

Don't know what I mean? Just watch:

> "Early on the first day of the week, while it was still dark, Mary Magdalene went to the tomb and saw that the stone had been removed from the entrance. So she came running to Simon Peter and the other disciple, the one Jesus loved, and said, 'They have taken the Lord out of the tomb, and we don't know where they have put him!'" John 20:1-2

Okay, so Mary wasn't racing anyone in that contest of one, but she ran nonetheless, going at full speed, eager to find someone who could help her find Jesus' body.

I live in Colorado where we're known for being active. Athletic gear is the norm, as is a person running down the road most any time of day. But in Jesus' day? I'm sure neither Mary's wardrobe or footwear prepared her for a morning sprint through town. Can't you just see the odd looks she caused as she passed by others, running as fast as she could until she got to the disciples?

Speaking of disciples, that's where the real race began. Let's back up a little to get the full context:

> "So she (Mary Magdalene) came running to Simon Peter and the other disciple, the one Jesus loved, and said, 'They have taken the Lord out of the tomb, and we don't know where they have put him!'
>
> So Peter and the other disciple started for the tomb. Both were running, but the other disciple outran Peter and reached the tomb first." John 20:2-3

I can't help but chuckle at my mental picture of this scene. First a woman sprints one way, then two men dash off in the direction she just came from, both trying to leave the other in their dust, and Mary being left far behind (it's okay, Mary. We know your race was double the distance).

I wish I could say Peter and John (here referred to as "the one Jesus loved") dashed off only for the purpose of confirming what Mary had said. I don't doubt that's what started them running, but I can just imagine one inching ahead just long enough for the other to kick it up a notch and run even faster.

What makes me envision it as a contest? For starters, I have a boy. My ten year old loves playing tag because he knows he's already faster than me. Plus, John inserts his bragging rights directly into the greatest climax ever: "Both were running, but the other disciple outran Peter and reached the tomb first."

Good job, John. We'll give you a virtual medal. But now, let's get back to what matters. It wasn't about *who* ran the race or who got there first. Rather, it was about *why* they ran.

Of course we know, but let's state the obvious: they ran with everything in them because they heard that something remarkable had happened.

By celebrating the same thing year after year, we run the risk of not running. Sure, we might run *to* the tomb to bask in the gift it offers, but we can overlook the starting line for the Easter races: that empty cave containing nothing more than folded up cloths.

Mary raced *away* from the tomb to tell others. Perhaps it's time we too heist our togas and sprint towards others to let them know how the emptiness of the tomb brings fullness to our lives.

PAUSE AND REFLECT

1. Take a few minutes to envision that first Easter race, especially as Mary neared the tomb and saw the stone rolled away. How do you think she felt? Do you think she understood what had happened?

2. I don't mean to, but my views of running seem to mirror my thoughts about telling others about Christ. I absolutely love to run and truly can't imagine not having that in my life, but I freely recognize that not everyone feels the same and I don't want to force my opinions on them. For those of you like me (even you non-runners), lets commit to doing something today whether in word or deed that shows the love of Christ to someone who doesn't yet understand the gift we've received.

3. Luke wrote, "However, I consider my life worth nothing to me; my only aim is to finish the race and complete the task the Lord Jesus has given me—the task of testifying to the good news of God's grace" (Acts 20:24). If you are able, wear tennis shoes today as a reminder of the race we're running and our task of testifying to the good news of God's grace.

DAY 42. A WHOLE WITH CRACKS

"Open this one carefully," my parents said one Christmas morning as they handed me a wrapped box. They perched on the edge of the couch, their anticipation rivaling their fear that I would break the contents.

I wanted to tear the paper to see what was inside, but instead I meticulously removed the green and red wrapping paper as if performing surgery. I lifted the lid off the box and saw pieces of glass in every shape and color.

"We know how much you enjoyed working on the class stained glass project, so we asked your art teacher if she would give you private lessons to make something on your own. She already cut the glass to match the design of the hot-air balloon you drew in class."

Since I knew exactly which drawing they were referring to, I didn't see just broken pieces of glass. I saw what they were designed to become—something to catch the light and make a beautiful display.

My teacher and I met once a week after school and began soldering the pieces together until the broken became a cohesive whole. Once completed, I hung what I made from my bedroom window so it could do exactly what stained glass is intended to do: let the light shine through in gorgeous ways.

Before walking to Calvary's tree, Jesus took the bread and said, "This is my body that is broken for you." It was only when that perfect, sinless body was broken that the holes in the earth could be shored up as the Holy Spirit came and infiltrated every heart that invited it in.

If I had tossed away the pieces of glass because they were broken and unkempt, I would have missed out on the beauty I eventually helped create. If I toss my life away, believing it is too broken, dirty, or shame-filled to approach the throne of grace, then I pretend that something that cost my Jesus everything was merely a year-end clearance item. What is worse, if I believe my brokenness disqualifies me from sharing the beauty of Easter with others—the enormity of Jesus' love poured out in a heart-wrenching, earth-shattering way—then the sacred work is nothing more than an ornamented tree.

The Liberty Bell cracked during a test strike. It was recast twice, yet a crack remains to this day. Rabbi Bradley Shavit Artson writes, "Looking at this magnificent bell I realized that this bell—cracked and silent—resonates more loudly around the globe than any bell that is whole."

It is no irony that part of Leviticus 25:10 is inscribed inside the Liberty Bell. "Proclaim liberty throughout the land, to all the inhabitants thereof."

Yes, you and I might be broken, but God's love shines even brighter through these cracks, giving us the compassion and the humility to loudly proclaim the unthinkable. We have huge gaping holes, yet the mercy of light breaking forth out of darkness makes us whole. Whole, with a few cracks highlighting love and mercy, that is.

PAUSE AND REFLECT

1. Have you ever worked with something that most would consider trash and made it new? If so, what was it and what was the final product? What did people say about your idea before you started and what was their response when you were done?

2. Do you feel like you're whole, broken, cracked with patches, or something in between? Why?

3. How are you doing at living out the inscription found inside the Liberty Bell? Do you proclaim liberty throughout the land, the freedom found only through Jesus' ultimate gift of love?

DAY 43. IT ENDS HERE

To some, the prayer request I posted in a private Facebook group seemed ludicrous. Others knew it contained something deep, although the words themselves didn't fully divulge that. The friends in that prayer circle who were closest to me understood exactly what I was requesting: a petition for freedom.

I had been in a long-term relationship with someone who chastised me for something without merit. At first I dismissed the accusations, but over time they began to sink in, distorting the way I viewed life, myself, and even the thing I felt most called to do.

More than a year after that relationship ended, I still battled against those deadly words. My brain knew without a doubt the fallacy in them, but my heart held on to a different reality. I tried time and time again to refute the myths, yet they continued to paralyze me. In a desperate attempt to eradicate the lies and fill my heart with God's truth, I reached out to my valiant prayer warriors.

It ends here, I told myself as I posted my odd sounding prayer request to the closed Facebook group.

"I know it sounds silly, but if you happen to see me, please remind me that it's okay to write at night after the kids go to bed."

A simple sentence, but a desperate plea. I longed for the freedom that can only come from God's truths penetrating my mind and heart.

I share something that might seem elementary, but that fear-filled place in my heart began to control me. Stuck between intellect and emotion, I was unable to fully savor the gift of abundant life. What you are now reading is a direct result of the encouragement and prayers of those faithful warriors.

While this example is unique to me, there is another crippling thought that is much too prevalent: believing that Jesus loved the world and gave His life as a blanket covering all of mankind but never accepting the gift of His personal kindness and love on an intimate level.

If that is you, let me urge you to do whatever it takes to shatter that head/heart disparity, for until you do, you will never be able to fully appreciate this most unthinkable and undeserving gift that Jesus gave you. If you fall into this trap, let it end here today.

PAUSE AND REFLECT

1. To some, the words "Jesus loves me" are a refrain from a Sunday school song, while others view them as a blanket covering the world. Some have it as their heart cry, and others fall somewhere in between. What about you? How does your head—and your heart!!—respond to the news of Jesus' love for you?

2. In the event that you lean towards believing that Jesus died for all of mankind without appreciating the individual gift He offers to each one of us, are you willing to let today be the day you stop believing this myth?

3. Think about a time someone inflicted intense pain on you. Was it intentional or accidental? Would you have endured it had you known how much it was going to hurt? On a scale of 1-10, how painful was it? Now compare that to the lashes Christ received, the thorns jabbed into His forehead, the asphyxiation He suffered as He could no longer breathe. What might that tell you about the depth of His love for you?

4. If you come to the place where you can say, “I know Jesus loves me on a personal and intimate level,” then I’m asking that from that moment forward you decide to stop letting Jesus’ love be a question. Instead, when you’re faced with doubts, remind yourself (out loud, if necessary) that you already wrestled with this question and declared God’s love as the victor. I can’t stress the importance of this enough because some of the greatest headway Satan can make in our lives is to convince us that we fall outside of the love and grace of God. Are you ready to take this challenge?

DAY 44. TWO DIFFERENT MEN, TWO DIFFERENT PATHS

Newton argued that for every reaction, there is an equal and opposite reaction. While it is true for quantum mechanics, it isn't always accurate for the human race. For example, two people can face a similar encounter. One will dig in and press on, while the other becomes bitter and resentful.

The events leading up to Jesus' arrest and during His trials are startling displays of this reality. One man stood to gain financially and therefore betrayed Christ. Another feared being arrested, mocked, or tortured himself so he denied even knowing Jesus. It is easily argued that the consequences of Judas' betrayal by far surpassed the effects of Peter's adamant denials that he knew Jesus. After all, Judas' acts led to Jesus' death, while Jesus' fate would not have changed if Peter had screamed far and wide that Jesus was innocent.

I'm not about to say the two events fall on the same plane, yet I'm keenly aware that the math of heaven doesn't always produce the same results as the arithmetic our teachers taught us.

Romans 6:23 says, "the wages of sin is death." After realizing that Jesus was condemned, Judas "was filled with remorse and returned the thirty pieces of silver to the chief priests and elders. 'I have sinned by betraying innocent blood,' he said" (Matthew 27:3b-4a). I tread lightly because I don't want to minimize what Judas did or give him too much credit, but there's a small part of me that admires the fact that in the end Judas was honest with himself and others: "I have sinned."

All too often I try to downplay what I've done rather than own it. But own it Judas did, and not in a way I'd ever recommend.

> "What is that to us?' they (the chief priests and elders) replied. 'You bear the responsibility.'
>
> So Judas threw the silver into the temple and left. **Then he went away and hanged himself**."
> Matthew 27:4b-5, emphasis mine

Contrast that to Peter. We know he denied Jesus, but listen in to the ways in which he did so:

> "Now Peter was sitting out in the courtyard, and a servant girl came to him. 'You also were with Jesus of Galilee,' she said.

But he denied it before them all. 'I don't know what you're talking about,' he said.

Then he went out to the gateway, where another servant girl saw him and said to the people there, 'This fellow was with Jesus of Nazareth.'

He denied it again, with an oath: 'I don't know the man!'

After a little while, those standing there went up to Peter and said, 'Surely you are one of them; your accent gives you away.'

Then he began to call down curses, and he swore to them, 'I don't know the man!'" (Matthew 26:69-74, emphasis mine)

There is little doubt that Peter had been near when Jesus previously said, "So everyone who acknowledges me before men, I also will acknowledge before my Father who is in heaven, but whoever denies me before men, I also will deny before my Father who is in heaven" (Matthew 10:32-33, ESV).

Let that sink in: Peter openly denied Jesus before others, which he knew meant that Jesus would deny him based on Matthew 10:32-33. In fact, Peter didn't just deny Jesus, he went on to call down curses (which I truly appreciate the censoring as we get direct quotes of Peter denying Jesus while only getting a generality of the curses). Peter undoubtedly would know that his life as a follower of Christ was over, and worse yet, his life beyond this life was too.

But like I said, the math of heaven is strange (gratefully so!). Watch this foreshadowing of extreme grace as the angels gave instructions to the women who discovered the empty tomb:

> "But go, tell His disciples and Peter, 'He is going ahead of you into Galilee. There you will see Him, just as He told you" (Mark 16:6)

"And Peter." A special phrase of inclusion for one who had already scratched his name off the roster.

Did he deserve being sought out to receive added heaps of grace? Based on the equation of Matthew 10:33, absolutely not.

Did he receive it? Most definitely.

It's time to flip the question.

Do we deserve it? Without a doubt, no.

Will we receive it? That is up to you and me.

PAUSE AND REFLECT

1. Think about a time when you denied Christ, either through your words or actions. How did you feel?

2. Did you feel comfortable praying and talking to God after doing whatever it was you answered in the question above?

3. Will you condemn yourself and believe that your sin is the one offense that can't be covered by the blood that Jesus shed? Or will you let the words, "And _____(insert your name)" be true for you as well?

DAY 45. I AM HEALED FULLY, THIS I KNOW

I told you a bit about my former boss's memorial service on Day 39, but there's a piece I chose not to mention until now: his slideshow. Friends compiled pictures of Doug doing many of the things he loved the most: fishing, hosting large gatherings of friends, and, of course, his family. As we watched images flash across the screen, the background music stopped and these words filled the void:

"I am healed fully, this I know."

It wasn't just any voice saying this, mind you. It was Doug. Truly. Like a voice from the other side, his tone echoed throughout the auditorium: I am healed.

No, it wasn't a ghost. Rather, Doug had chosen to preach at his church about a month or so prior to his passing. It was recorded in advance since talking was a strain for him at that point as he needed to press against his tracheotomy tube in order for the words to come out clearly.

He spoke of many things, including his refusal to ever give the impression that God had abandoned him, about wanting his kids to look back on his journey and see that he went through it but never lost faith in what God's ultimate plan was for him. That was the first time I heard the shift in his perspective as he spoke less of what would happen once he beat cancer and instead said, "According to the doctors, this is not going to turn out well for me." And then the recorded words from his sermon rang out during his service:

"I am healed ultimately already. There's no getting away from that so with that in my back pocket I can go forward every day. I am healed fully. This I know."

Friend, that can be our chant as well. Yes, we face unthinkable things in this life. Some of you might be battling cancer or have lost someone dear to you after that fight. Others are struggling to pay the bills. Our list could go on and on. But here's a truth that rocks me to my core: Thomas, one of the disciples, said after Jesus' resurrection, "Unless I see the nail marks in his hands and put my finger where the nails were, and put my hand into his side, I will not believe" (John 20: 25b).

Later, when Jesus came to the disciples, He said to Thomas, "Put your finger here; see my hands. Reach out your hand and put it into my side" (John 20:27a).

Yes, after the resurrection, Jesus had wounds from the nails that were driven into His hands and feet and on His side after being pierced with a sword. That makes sense to me since those wounds had been inflicted only a few days before. Theologians believe those scars will always remain and we'll see them clearly when we get to heaven.

My marks will be wiped away. The scar on my face where a dog scratched me will be gone. So will the scars from the incisions they made to take out my gallbladder. I imagine Doug will probably be fishing and won't need a trach anymore.

But Jesus?

His scars will remain.

PAUSE AND REFLECT

1. Doug's wife graciously allowed me to share the links to his sermon and service. I encourage you to watch either of them, for they both are a call to life—to embrace this beautiful gift we've been given—while they also remind us of the suffering from which we are not immune. To find his sermon, simply google "Doug Wittenberg sermon." His memorial service can be found at www.vimeo.com/211063678. The password is Doug.

2. Friend, don't take this lightly. We are healed—and that isn't something that is promised only after we die. I'm not saying our physical trials will end solely by believing in God. The price has been paid and we don't

need to keep expecting ourselves to earn it. Let the healing run deep.

3. What impact does it have on you that Jesus will forever have scars—the very ones He bore for you and me? What does that tell you about His love, mercy and forgiveness?

DAY 46. FOR THE LOVE OF INJUSTICE

I'm a lover of justice, one of those people who never outgrew the "it's not fair" whine. I can't stand hearing about cold cases because I want the person who committed a crime off the streets and closure for the families of the victim. Every week I make a list of chores then divide them equally between my kids so they can't claim it's not fair if one has more to do than the other.

For as much as I love justice, I also love the lack of it when it falls on me. It's hard for me to accept when I've been judged to be guilty of something. It goes against my grain and I am faced with the challenge of receiving, embracing, and releasing it.

Let me demonstrate:

Barabbas, the notorious criminal who they knew was guilty, was released.

The guilty walked away without any consequence.

If it seems unfair, well, it is. Let's celebrate how very unfair a verdict of innocence is when knowing full well we're guilty!

PAUSE AND REFLECT

1. Do you fall more into the pursuit of justice category or are you a lover of grace?

2. For my fellow justice crew, think about the extreme *lack* of justice we've received from God because of what Christ did, taking all of our sins upon Himself so that we can be pronounced clean. For those of you that are more bent towards grace, take time to thank God for showing grace to you, which has allowed you to do the same for others.

3. Injustice can seem so unfair, yet hopefully we all know firsthand how beneficial it is when we receive it. Today, let's live the resurrection by asking God if there are people to whom we need to extend a *lack* of justice. Perhaps we need to release a hurt that has weighed us down. Sure, it isn't fair to seemingly let the other person off the hook, but neither is it fair to keep yourself bound to that anchor.

DAY 47. THE COURAGE TO DOUBT

"Because I said so."

Anyone who has been a regular recipient of this age-old adage knows it doesn't do much in terms of building trust. This response is appropriate occasionally, such as when kids ask about something beyond their years. However, most times it's said as a way to avoid explaining and instead gives a pass to bark orders.

"Clean your room. Now!"

"Why does it need to be done now? Can't it wait until after I finish eating dinner?"

And then comes the trust-shattering response: "because I said so!"

There are many instances of Jesus saying, "You have heard it said," but nowhere is it recorded that He told someone to do something "because He said so."

In fact, Jesus seems to accept our doubts. Take Thomas, for example, who is best known for saying, "Unless I see the nail marks in His hands and put my finger where the nails were, and put my hand into His side, I will not believe" (John 20:25).

When Jesus saw Thomas, He said, "Because you have seen me, you have believed; blessed are those who have not seen and yet have believed" (John 20:29).

Jesus seems to accept our doubts.

While there seems to be a dichotomy between those who didn't believe (Thomas) and those who did, Jesus did not chastise Thomas for doubting. After all, Jesus died and then came back to life. Let's be real: that's a pretty hard thing to accept.

In fact, some did not. A rumor spread attempting to refute the resurrection as soldiers claimed someone stole Jesus' body. Matthew records it this way:

> "While the women were on their way, some of the guards went into the city and reported to the chief priests everything that had happened. When the chief priests had met with the elders and devised a plan, they gave the soldiers a large sum of money, telling them, "You are to say, 'His disciples came during the night and stole him away while we were asleep.' If this report gets to the governor, we will satisfy him and keep you out of trouble." So the soldiers took the money and did as they were instructed. And this story has been widely circulated among the Jews to this very day." Matthew 28:11-15

Just as Jesus didn't condemn Thomas for doubting, there isn't any condemnation if you believe the stolen-body myth, but in the event you do, let's break it down for a minute.

I originally typed out a response describing the soldiers who feared that Jesus' body would be stolen and received an order to seal the tomb. I conjectured about how someone could roll away the stone without the watch of guards noticing.

But you know what? It felt a lot like a "because I told you so" response. Even though I deleted it, I'm sorry because this girl has many questions too. I'm sure my questions are different than yours, but here's the beautiful truth: regardless of what our questions are, we don't have to be scared about asking them. Jesus still entered the room, even knowing a doubting Thomas was there. He still said, "my peace be with you" to all of the disciples, including Thomas.

Doubt does not disqualify.

Friend, we're nearly done with our time together. We'll have a few more challenges of how to reflect the resurrection in our lives, but first we must admit any doubts we might have, for it is only then we can say, "I believe. Help my unbelief" (Mark 9:24).

PAUSE AND REFLECT

1. What are your thoughts about doubt? Do you think they're okay, do you think they offend God, or do you fall somewhere in between?

2. Do you have scripture to back up your answer to the question above? If not, take some time to look for some. Biblegateway.com or GotQuestions.org are good starting points.

3. If you found scriptures regarding doubt, how do they challenge your views? What does Jesus' response to Thomas tell you about doubt? Is it a sign of weakness, courage, or something in between? More importantly, what does it say about our ability to voice our doubts to God?

4. Are there any doubts you've held on to but have been too scared to address? Let me challenge you to tell God about them (besides, I'm pretty sure He already knows about them).

DAY 48. THE RACES CONTINUE

Not long after the resurrection, our two competitive chaps from the Easter races are back at it. Let's first set the stage:

> "Afterward Jesus appeared again to his disciples, by the Sea of Galilee. It happened this way: Simon Peter, Thomas (also known as Didymus), Nathanael from Cana in Galilee, the sons of Zebedee, and two other disciples were together. 'I'm going out to fish,' Simon Peter told them, and they said, 'We'll go with you.' So they went out and got into the boat, but that night they caught nothing.
>
> Early in the morning, Jesus stood on the shore, but the disciples did not realize that it was Jesus.

He called out to them, 'Friends, haven't you any fish?'

'No,' they answered.

He said, 'Throw your net on the right side of the boat and you will find some.' When they did, they were unable to haul the net in because of the large number of fish. " John 21:1-6

Here comes the starting line of this race:

"Then the disciple whom Jesus loved said to Peter, 'It is the Lord!' As soon as Simon Peter heard him say, 'It is the Lord,' he wrapped his outer garment around him (for he had taken it off) and jumped into the water." John 20:7

Okay John, you disciple whom Jesus loved, we'll give you another pretend medal for recognizing Jesus first. Beyond that, this one goes to Peter for grabbing his clothes and jumping into the water to get to shore faster (if it were me, I might have taken a layer of clothes off to go faster rather than adding them on, but hey, whatever works).

I love this scene. The men's gloominess over an unsuccessful fishing trip flipped when they realized Jesus was in their midst. Acknowledging Jesus wasn't a simple, "Hey man. How've you been?" Nope! After all, we're talking about the very one who had died and rose again.

Peter was a fisherman, so he knew the cardinal rule: don't abandon your boat or nets. That would be like me leaving my laptop with all of my writing stored on it at Starbucks or my kids at the grocery store (although I must admit that one is tempting sometimes).

But that didn't matter. Peter abandoned all of it to race towards what was most important.

Jesus.

Friends, we can only reflect what is close to us. If we're going to reflect the resurrection to others, then we also need to race towards Jesus and be eager to spend time in His presence.

PAUSE AND REFLECT

1. Look back on John 20:1-6. When did Peter start fishing and what time of day did Jesus appear? Are you more or less excited to be around other people after working a long shift or being exhausted?

2. Think about what Peter must have looked like when he made it to Jesus: tired from working all night, wet from jumping in the water, and there was probably a smell attached to him from both. Many times we convince ourselves that we need to have our stuff

together before approaching Jesus. How does the way Peter presented himself challenge that notion?

3. Today let's adopt an "it's Jesus attitude." Race towards Him, regardless of where you are physically or spiritually. Get excited to spend some time with Jesus.

DAY 49. DYING AMONG THE LIVING

We know that the women went to the tomb early on the first morning of the week with the spices they had prepared for Jesus' body. They found the stone rolled away and went inside the tomb (no small thing, considering that John even admits to waiting outside rather than going in) and wondered what happened to the body of Jesus. Then "suddenly two men in clothes that gleamed like lightning stood beside them. In their fright the women bowed down with their faces to the ground but the men said to them, 'Why do you look for the living among the dead?'" (Luke 24:4-6).

I don't hear judgment in the angel's voices. In fact, rather than criticizing them, they went on to remind the women of what Jesus had said:

> "He is not here; he has risen! Remember how he told you, while he was still with you in Galilee: The Son of Man must be delivered into the hands

of sinful men, be crucified and on the third day be raised again." Luke 24:6-7

With that explanation came remembrance: "Then they remembered his words" (Luke 24: 8).

As I read these words this morning, a thought struck me: what if the angels were to ask us in that same gentle and non-judgmental manner why we die among the living?

Can't you just see the expressions of bewilderment on our faces? *What do you mean?* we might ask. *I'm not six feet under yet. I'm alive.* At that point we too might receive a reminder, one as gentle as the one given inside the empty tomb: Don't you remember what Jesus said, that He came so you might have life, and to have it to the full? Why, then, do you hang onto your hurts and refuse to release them? Why do you act as if you are worth so little when someone gave His very life for you?

Like I said, I'm conjecturing here. There is no recorded evidence of angels saying these words to someone although Jesus' words regarding abundant life can be found in John 10:10.

The cross serves as a reminder of the power of death—and of a power that is stronger than death. In this season of remembrance, let me offer one as well:

Live.

Live abundantly, my friend. Yes, there are seasons where such a luxury seems unthinkable, but even during those times, be careful not to die among the living rather than living life to the full.

PAUSE AND REFLECT

1. What kind of tone do you think the angels used towards the women in the tomb? Do you think they were critical, judgmental, loving, and/or instructional? What part of the Scripture makes you think that?

2. Do you believe there are some Christians who are dying among the living? If so, how do they exhibit that kind of death?

3. Is there anything in your life that might make others characterize you as dying more than living? This is asked in more of an emotional sense as opposed to physical limitations such as getting older, battling cancer or anything else.

4. How does Christ's ultimate gift, given so that "they might have life and have it to the full" challenge the

way you come and go? Is there anything you need to ask Jesus to transform your living and thinking?

DAY 50. REFLECTING EASTER

A reflection mirrors something else, allowing us to peer at what we otherwise can't see. Just like I stand in front of a full-length mirror to gain a perspective on my outfit that I wouldn't have by just looking down, the way we live can serve as a reflection of Christ's love and ultimate sacrifice, giving others the chance to see Him in a way they otherwise could not.

Let's just stop and catch our breath. I mean, seriously, that's a tall order to have our lives reflect something so grand.

But that's precisely it: it *is* something grand. It's extraordinary and is too remarkable to live as if it is anything but. So while a life of reflection is huge, a life lived that *doesn't* reflect that love minimizes the gift and becomes an unconscious way of saying that the ultimate sacrifice was just okay.

Years ago, a friend wrote a song about being moon people. Just as the moon reflects the sun's light, his lyrics were a challenge for us to be moon people reflecting the Son's light. It's no small challenge, but it was no small sacrifice. Sign me up.

Another friend believes the best way for our reflection to fade is to strip away our joy and live in the doldrums. As I've pondered her words for the past few months, I've come to agree. After all, who is drawn to someone who can only find the bad in any situation?

Don't get me wrong: I fiercely believe life can be gruelingly hard. I'm not about to paint a portrait of Jesus skipping to the cross, but hear this:

> "Therefore, since we are surrounded by such a great cloud of witnesses, let us throw off everything that hinders and the sin that so easily entangles. And let us run with perseverance the race marked out for us, fixing our eyes on Jesus, the pioneer and perfecter of faith. **For the joy set before him he endured the cross,** scorning its shame, and sat down at the right hand of the throne of God." Hebrews 12:1-2, emphasis mine

Christ's joy wasn't in the pain of the cross. Rather, He endured it for the sake of the great joy He knew would come from it. He also knew that a direct result of his pain was that you, me, and countless others could join him in paradise.

If you've been on my blog or read any of my Facebook posts, you'll know I've been dubbed the gratitude girl, in large part based on a word I coined: gratimoment, which simply means moments of gratitude. This word was birthed in me as I studied contentment and learned about the radical effects of gratitude. I knew I couldn't be grateful all the time, but I could choose to intentionally carve out moments of gratitude.

Yes, there are countless benefits of an attitude of gratitude: health benefits, employment benefits, benefits to employers. But today let's look at the benefit it provides to others: the benefit of reflecting.

Let me repeat something radical: "For the joy set before him . . . " (Hebrews 12:2). This is our challenge. If Jesus could endure something as horrific as the cross for the sake of *joy*, then shouldn't we be able to express a little joy in our lives?

I'll be the first to admit my life doesn't always make it easy to do so, but I'm also trying. Desperately trying.

So to all of us I say *shine on*! Let your joy shine bright. Share the greatest story ever lived every day in your words and actions. And for the sake of the glory of the cross, embrace joy and never, ever let anyone take that from you.

PAUSE AND REFLECT

1. How joyful would some of your closet friends say you are? I'm not asking if life is peachy or if you are

apt to stick your head in the coffee grounds and act as if everything is okay. My question is more about the level of happiness we exhibit to others or the deep-seated faith we might have, even when things are rough. No one is reading your answers or grading your response, so there's no need to pretend.

2. How well does your answer above stack up to the incredible gift of eternal life we've been offered—a gift given at the ultimate cost? How can you make the two better line up together if they don't already?

3. Reread the words at the top of the section, for that is our challenge right now: Pause. Reflect. Carve out some time today and in the coming days to reflect. Think about the cross and the amazing gift it offers you. Reflect on what your life might look like if it weren't for that incredible gift. And then, think about how you can best reflect—reflect the love and *joy!* of Christ to others.

OTHER BOOKS IN THIS SERIES:

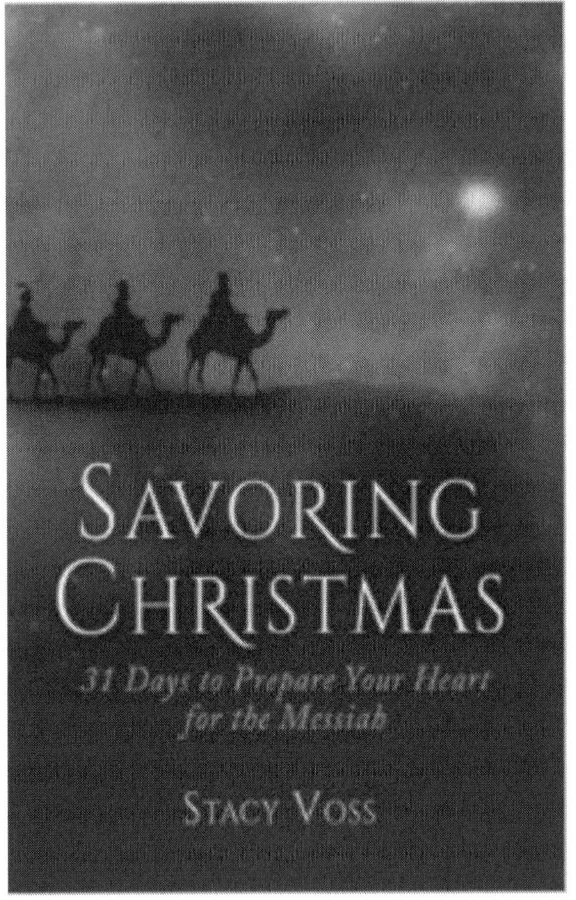

Savoring Christmas: Available on Amazon, Kindle, and Nook

Embracing Thanksgiving: publication date pending